Contents

D0179137

How to use this book

Each page has a title telling you what it is about.

Instructions look like this. Always read these carefully before starting.

This shows you how to set out your work. The first question is done for you.

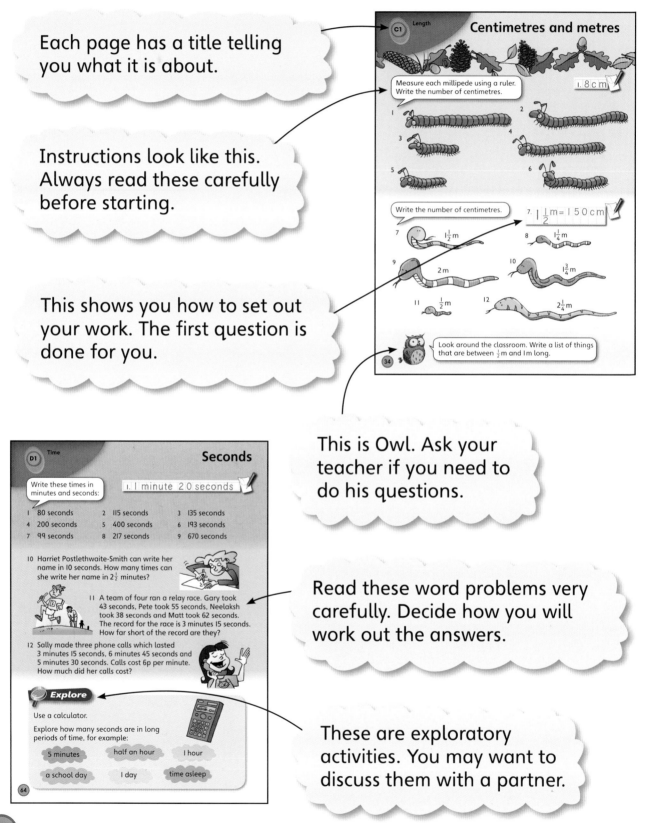

This is Owl. Ask your teacher if you need to do his questions.

Read these word problems very carefully. Decide how you will work out the answers.

These are exploratory activities. You may want to discuss them with a partner.

Hundreds, tens and units

Write each number in figures.

1. 5 6 1

1 five hundred and sixty-one

2 one hundred and ninety-nine

3 two hundred and fifty-three

4 four hundred and seventy-two

5 six hundred and six

6 nine hundred and thirty-seven

Write each number in words.

7. three hundred and sixty-five

7 365

8 402

9 279

10 543

11 612

12 187

Make the three largest 3-digit numbers possible using the rocket count-down numbers: '9, 8, 7, 6, 5, 4, 3, 2, 1, blast off!'

4-digit numbers

Write each number in figures.

1. | 1 | 6 | 4 | 7 |

1 one thousand, six hundred and forty-seven

2 three thousand, two hundred and sixty-one

3 six thousand, four hundred and seventy

4 two thousand and eighty-nine

5 five thousand and five

6 three thousand, six hundred and one

7 seven thousand, seven hundred and seven

8 four thousand, three hundred

Write the number before and the number after.

9. | 6 | 4 | 1 | 6 |, | 6 | 4 | 1 | 7 |, | 6 | 4 | 1 | 8 |

9 6417

10 2399

11 4001

12 5670

13 1999

14 1011

How many numbers between 100 and 10 000 have all their digits the same? Write them all.

4-digit numbers

Write the number made by adding the cards.

1. 6 4 7 0

1 6 0 0 0 4 0 0 7 0

2 3 0 0 0 1 0 0 9 0 1

3 4 0 0 0 8 0 0 6 0 2

4 9 0 0 0 9 0 0 1 0

5 1 0 0 0 2 0 0

6 8 0 0 0 7 0 0 7 0

7 4 0 0 0 6 0 0

8 5 0 0 0 7 0 0 9 0 1

Write each number in words.

9. two thousand and one

9 2001

10 3300

11 4014

12 3003

13 6100

14 1099

Think of two 4-digit numbers, for example 4000 and 2000.
Ask your partner to write the number halfway between.

5

4-digit and 5-digit numbers

Write the dates one century earlier and one century later.

1. | 1 | 4 | 6 | 4 | , | 1 | 6 | 6 | 4 |

1 1564

2 1066

3 1492

4 1666

5 1812

6 1966

Think of a date in the last century you remember as important. Write the date 1000 years later, 2000 years later, 3000 years later and so on. Ask your partner to do the same.

Write each number in figures.

7. | 5 | 5 | , | 6 | 4 | 2 |

7 Fifty-five thousand, six hundred and forty-two

8 Seventy-two thousand, four hundred and sixty-four

9 Eighty-four thousand, nine hundred and thirty-three

10 Thirty-six thousand, seven hundred and twenty-eight

11 Forty-seven thousand, five hundred and nineteen

12 Sixty-six thousand, three hundred and ninety-seven

3-digit numbers

Put the cards together and write the number.

1. `3 4 2`

1. `3 0 0` `4 0` `2`

2. `4 0 0` `8 0` `9`

3. `6 0 0` `6 0` `6`

4. `7 0 0` `2`

5. `2 0 0` `9 0` `3`

6. `7 0 0` `1 0` `7`

7. `2 0 0` `4`

8. `5 0 0` `6 0` `5`

9. `9 0 0` `5 0` `3`

10. `8 0 0` `4 0` `8`

Write each number on three separate cards.

11. `4 0 0` `6 0` `7`

11. 467

12. 931

13. 784

14. 697

Use cards to make some palindromic numbers (numbers that read the same forwards and backwards). Ask your partner to make some as well.

`3 0 0` `6 0` `3`

4-digit and 5-digit numbers

Break each number into thousands, hundreds, tens and units.

1. 45 thousands
   3 hundreds
   4 tens
   6 units

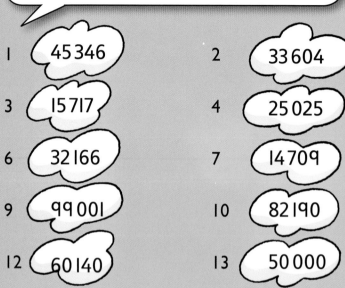

1. 45 346
2. 33 604
3. 15 717
4. 25 025
5. 60 105
6. 32 166
7. 14 709
8. 71 880
9. 99 001
10. 82 190
11. 10 010
12. 60 140
13. 50 000
14. 96 609

Write each number in figures.

15. 6 0,0 0 4

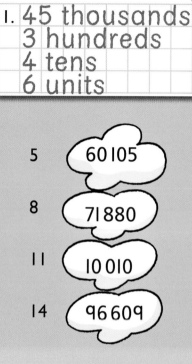

15   sixty thousand and four

16   seventeen thousand, six hundred and two

17   eighty thousand, four hundred and twenty

18   ninety-six thousand and forty-seven

19   nineteen thousand, nine hundred and nineteen

Add a teen number to the same number of thousands, e.g. 13 013. Write more numbers like this.

4-digit and 5-digit numbers

Write the dates 10 years later, 100 years later and 1000 years later.

1. 1463, 1473, 1563, 2463

1	1463	2	1984	3	1536

4	1889	5	1924	6	1912

7	2015	8	1648	9	1946

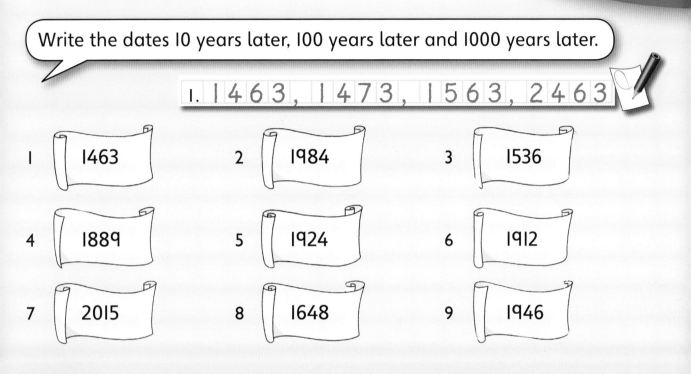

Work with a partner. Write some dates in the past which use each of the digits 9, 1, and 2. How many can you make?

Write each number in words.

1. sixty-six thousand and six

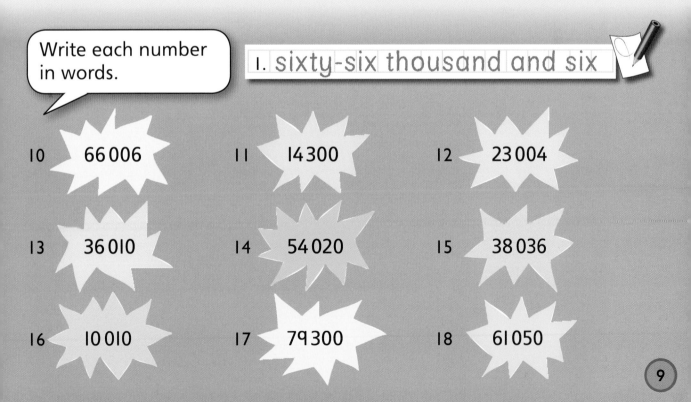

10	66 006	11	14 300	12	23 004

13	36 010	14	54 020	15	38 036

16	10 010	17	79 300	18	61 050

4-digit and 5-digit numbers

1

Use the place-value cards below to make 5-digit numbers. You must use five cards each time. There are 32 possible numbers – how many can you find?

50 000	90 000	1000	9
30	800	300	90
1	7000		

Make six 5-digit numbers using the cards. You don't have to use five cards for each number.

Which numbers match which clues?

2 All the digits are even.

3 The 10s digit is three times the 100s digit.

4 The digits are consecutive numbers.

5 The total of the digits is 10.

6 The number of 1000s is double the number of 100s.

7 The number has the same digit in the 10s place as in the 100s place.

9305   3412

4268   1553

1234

2846

6305

3396

Find some other numbers for each of these clues.

Multiplying

How many beakers in each set?

1. $3 \times 3 = 9$

Draw a grid to match each multiplication. Write the number of squares.

7. $3 \times 4 = 12$

7 3×4

8 2×5

9 4×5

10 6×2

11 5×5

12 3×10

13 2×2

14 9×2

Write multiplications to match different square grids, e.g. $4 \times 4 = 16$

Multiplying

How many stickers on each sheet?

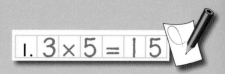
1. $3 \times 5 = 15$

1

2

3

4

5

6

7

8

9

Draw and label two grids that match each number.

10.

$3 \times 4 = 12 \qquad 4 \times 3 = 12$

10 12

11 20

12 15

13 6

How many grids can you draw that have 24 squares?

Multiplying

Copy and complete.

1. $3 \times 10 = 30$

1 $3 \times 10 = \boxed{}$

2 $2 \times 5 = \boxed{}$

3 $10 \times 6 = \boxed{}$

4 $4 \times 5 = \boxed{}$

5 $7 \times 2 = \boxed{}$

6 $3 \times 3 = \boxed{}$

7 $8 \times 5 = \boxed{}$

8 $1 \times 1 = \boxed{}$

9 $5 \times 7 = \boxed{}$

10 $3 \times 4 = \boxed{}$

11 $10 \times 10 = \boxed{}$

12 $20 \times 5 = \boxed{}$

13 Biscuits cost 7p. How much change will you have from 50p if you buy 5 biscuits?

14 Kevin the kangaroo travels 6 m with every hop. How far will he have gone after 25 hops?

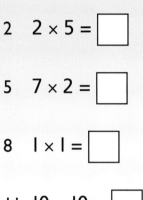

15 Raffle tickets cost 30p each. A book of 5 tickets costs £1·35. How much do you save by buying the book?

16 3 times a number is half of 5×6. What is the number?

$\boxed{} \times \boxed{} \times \boxed{} = 24$. What could the three numbers be? (Two might be the same.)

Multiplying

Two consecutive (next-door) numbers are multiplied together. These are the answers. What are the two numbers?

1. $3 \times 4 = 12$

1 12   2 20   3 2   4 30   5 90   6 6

What other answers could there be?

Write the missing numbers:

7   $3 \times \boxed{} = 18$

8   $2 \times \boxed{} = 14$

9   $\boxed{} \times 3 = 12$

10   $\boxed{} \times 5 = 40$

11   $7 \times \boxed{} = 70$

12   $6 \times \boxed{} = 30$

13   $\boxed{} \times 5 = 25$

14   $\boxed{} \times 4 = 28$

Invent 10 missing number multiplications which have answers from 1 to 10.

True or false? When two numbers are multiplied together:

15 If they are both less than 6, the answer is less than 25.

16 If one is odd and the other is even, the answer could be odd or even.

17 If they are both odd the answer is odd.

18 If one is a multiple of 5, the answer is a multiple of 5.

19 If they are both even the answer is even.

Dividing

Write a division to match each set.

1. $15 \div 5 = 3$

1

2

3

4

5

6

Copy and complete these divisions.

7. $14 \div 2 = 7$

7 $14 \div 2 = \boxed{}$

8 $15 \div 3 = \boxed{}$

9 $40 \div 10 = \boxed{}$

10 $40 \div 4 = \boxed{}$

11 $25 \div 5 = \boxed{}$

12 $18 \div 2 = \boxed{}$

13 $\boxed{} \div 5 = 3$

14 $21 \div 3 = \boxed{}$

15 $\boxed{} \div 10 = 6$

16 $6 \div 6 = \boxed{}$

17 $\boxed{} \div 1 = 8$

18 $16 \div 4 = \boxed{}$

Write eight different divisions that all have an answer of 5.

Write two divisions to match each set of tiles.

1. $20 \div 5 = 4$
$20 \div 4 = 5$

1
2
3
4

5
6

Draw some sets of tiles from which only one division can be written.

Class 4 has 27 children, who need to be split into teams. Write how many teams can be made, and how many children are left over.

7. $27 \div 3 = 9$ teams exactly

7
teams of 3

8
teams of 4

9
teams of 2

10
teams of 10

11
teams of 5

12
teams of 6

Find different ways of splitting 24 children into teams of equal size, with no children left over.

Dividing

Use each list to help you complete these divisions with remainders.

1. $15 \div 4 = 3 \text{ r } 3$

| 4 | 8 | 12 | 16 | 20 | 24 | 28 | 32 | 36 | 40 |

1   $15 \div 4$ 2 $29 \div 4$ 3 $38 \div 4$ 4 $22 \div 4$

| 5 | 10 | 15 | 20 | 25 | 30 | 35 | 40 | 45 | 50 |

5   $23 \div 5$ 6 $18 \div 5$ 7 $44 \div 5$ 8 $36 \div 5$

The lists for 4s and the lists for 5s have two numbers in common: 20 and 40. Find some other pairs of lists that have numbers in common.

9. $13 \div 3 = 4 \text{ r } 1$
    5 chairs

How many chair lifts are needed for:

9   13 people   10   22 people   11   28 people

Chair lifts 3 people only

How many cable cars are need for:

12   21 people   13   43 people   14   82 people

Cable cars 4 people only

How many toboggans are needed for:

15   17 people   16   28 people   17   61 people

Toboggans 5 people only

What number of people can fit exactly into chair lifts, into cable cars and into toboggans?

Dividing

1. true

True or false?

1. $18 \div 4 = 4 \text{ r } 2$

2. $21 \div 5 = 4 \text{ r } 1$

3. $36 \div 10 = 6 \text{ r } 3$

4. $25 \div 3 = 8 \text{ r } 2$

5. $23 \div 2 = 11 \text{ r } 1$

6. $38 \div 4 = 8 \text{ r } 2$

7. $26 \div 3 = 8 \text{ r } 2$

8. $43 \div 5 = 9 \text{ r } 3$

9. $25 \div 4 = 6 \text{ r } 1$

Rewrite the false ones with the correct answer.

10. Five friends go for a burger. The bill comes to £16. If each person paid with £5, how much change would they each receive?

11. Ashok tidies his bricks by storing them in piles of 4. He has 38 bricks. How many piles does he make?

12. Jenny eats 4 slices of toast every day. A loaf has 17 slices. How many days will they last?

13. Mel is saving to buy 5p stickers. She has enough money to buy 7 stickers and have 3p left over. How much has she saved?

Explore

7 gives a remainder of 1 when divided by both 2 and 3.
$7 \div 2 = 3 \text{ r } 1$ $7 \div 3 = 2 \text{ r } 1$

Find other numbers that also give a remainder of 1 when divided by both 2 and 3.

Find numbers that give a remainder of 1 when divided by both 2 and 5.

Number pairs

Write the length missing from each metre stick.

1. 75 cm

1   25 cm

2   30 cm

3   15 cm

4   45 cm

5   65 cm

6   5 cm

7   85 cm

8   10 cm

9   55 cm

10   35 cm

Copy and complete.

11. 30 + 70 = 100

11   30 + ⬤ = 100

12   25 + ⬤ = 100

13   100 − 35 = ⬤

14   40 + ⬤ = 100

15   55 + ⬤ = 100

16   85 + ⬤ = 100

17   100 − 5 = ⬤

18   20 + ⬤ = 100

19   100 − 45 = ⬤

20   100 − 10 = ⬤

Write a pair of numbers which add to 10.
Your partner writes a different pair making 10.
Continue like this. Who runs out of pairs first?

19

Number pairs

How much further for each walker to reach 1 km?

1. $300m + 700m = 1000m$

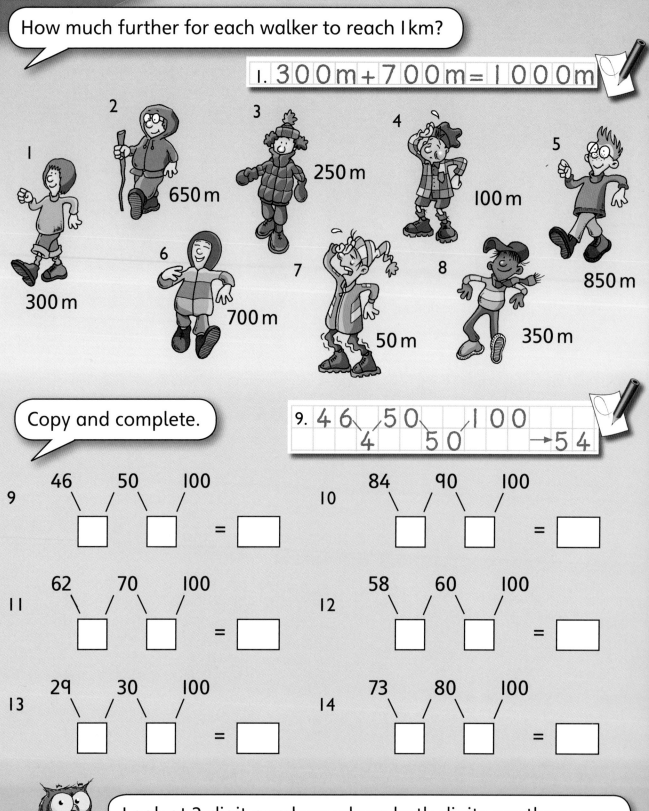

2. 650 m

3. 250 m

1. 300 m

4. 100 m

5. 850 m

6. 700 m

7. 50 m

8. 350 m

Copy and complete.

9.
| 4 6 | 5 0 | | 1 0 0 | |
| 4 | | 5 0 | | →5 4 |

9
| 46 | 50 | 100 |

□ □ = □

10
| 84 | 90 | 100 |

□ □ = □

11
| 62 | 70 | 100 |

□ □ = □

12
| 58 | 60 | 100 |

□ □ = □

13
| 29 | 30 | 100 |

□ □ = □

14
| 73 | 80 | 100 |

□ □ = □

Look at 2-digit numbers where both digits are the same.
Write the matching pair to make 100. Is there a pattern?

Number pairs

Pairs of cards make 100. Write the number on the blank card.

1. 62 70 100
   8   30   →38

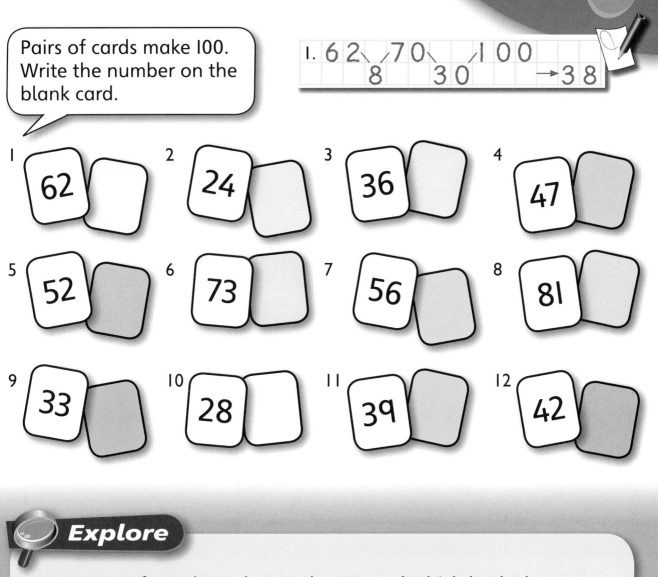

1. 62
2. 24
3. 36
4. 47
5. 52
6. 73
7. 56
8. 81
9. 33
10. 28
11. 39
12. 42

Explore

Write pairs of numbers that make 100 and which both share a digit, for example, 73 + 27 or 64 + 36. How many can you find?

Copy and complete.

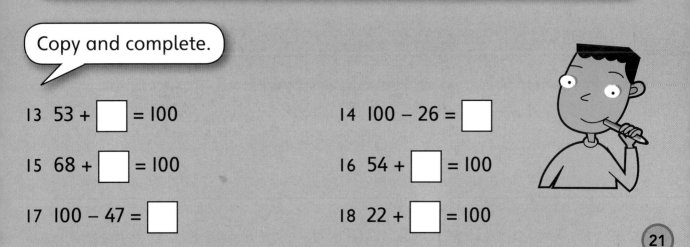

13. $53 + \boxed{} = 100$

14. $100 - 26 = \boxed{}$

15. $68 + \boxed{} = 100$

16. $54 + \boxed{} = 100$

17. $100 - 47 = \boxed{}$

18. $22 + \boxed{} = 100$

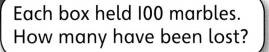
Number pairs

Each box held 100 marbles. How many have been lost?

1.	6 4	7 0		1 0 0	
		6	3 0		→ 3 6

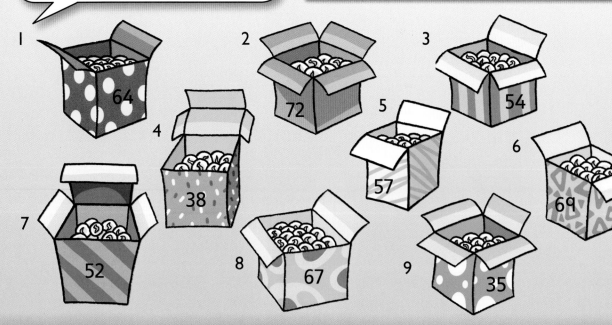

1. 64
2. 72
3. 54
4. 38
5. 57
6. 69
7. 52
8. 67
9. 35

Can you find two 2-digit numbers that add to 100 and whose four digits do not add to 19? What is the rule for those that do not add to 19?

10 Sunil has 100 conkers. He gives 34 to his younger sister. How many does he have left?

11 Mrs Sums has 100 stickers. She uses 27 in an assembly. How many does she have left?

12 Tom pays 36p for his ice-cream, using a £1 coin. How much change does he have? Suppose he buys two ice-creams?

13 There are 100 pens in a box. 47 are red and the rest are blue. How many are blue?

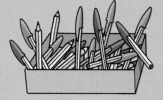

Number pairs

Write the change from £1.

1. $100p - 59p = 41p$

1	2	3	4	5	6
59p	27p	68p	18p	73p	66p

7	8	9	10	11	12
55p	83p	33p	44p	75p	65p

Find the fewest coins you need to give change for each ice-cream.

Copy and complete.

13. $£1·36 + 64p = £2$

13 $£1·36 + \boxed{}p = £2$

14 $£2·24 + \boxed{} = £3$

15 $£4·42 + \boxed{} = £5$

16 $£5·35 + \boxed{} = £6$

17 $£6·73 + \boxed{} = £7$

18 $£8·56 + \boxed{} = £9$

23

Number pairs

How many centimetres to the next metre?

1. $346\,cm + 54\,cm = 4\,m$

5 m

6 464 cm

7 437 cm

5 428 cm

8 417 cm

3 372 cm

4 357 cm

4 m

1 346 cm

2 338 cm

Write a palindromic number between 200 and 300, e.g. 242. How much must be added to get to 300? Repeat this, looking for the patterns.

Write the amount cut off each ribbon.

9. $381\,cm + 19\,cm = 4\,m$

9

was 4 m, now 381 cm

10

was 6 m, now 555 cm

11

was 3 m, now 274 cm

12

was 8 m, now 737 cm

Number pairs

How many more metres to the next kilometre?

1. $3500m + 500m = 4km$

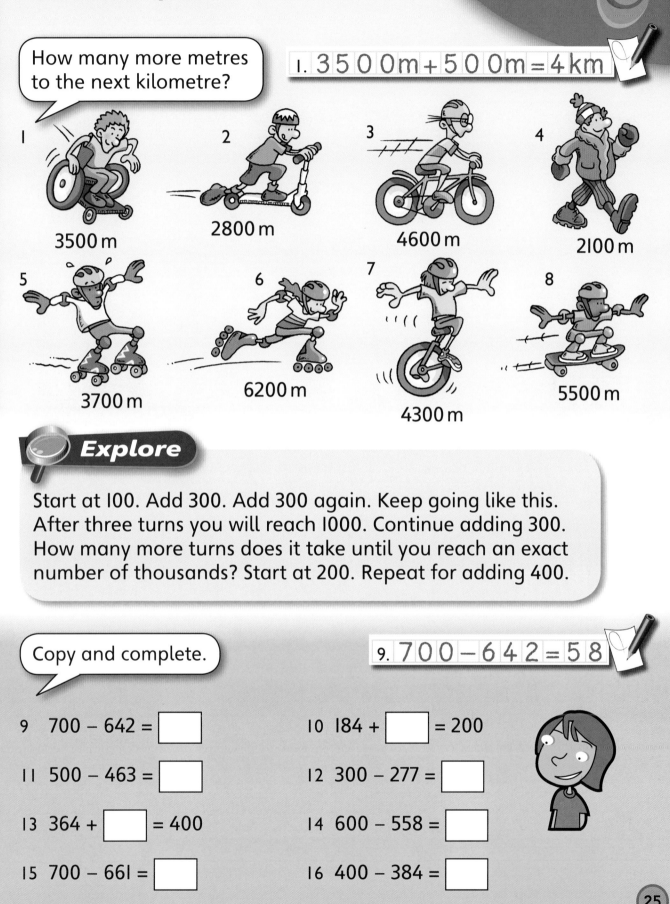

1. 3500 m
2. 2800 m
3. 4600 m
4. 2100 m
5. 3700 m
6. 6200 m
7. 4300 m
8. 5500 m

Explore

Start at 100. Add 300. Add 300 again. Keep going like this. After three turns you will reach 1000. Continue adding 300. How many more turns does it take until you reach an exact number of thousands? Start at 200. Repeat for adding 400.

Copy and complete.

9. $700 - 642 = 58$

9 $700 - 642 = \boxed{}$

10 $184 + \boxed{} = 200$

11 $500 - 463 = \boxed{}$

12 $300 - 277 = \boxed{}$

13 $364 + \boxed{} = 400$

14 $600 - 558 = \boxed{}$

15 $700 - 661 = \boxed{}$

16 $400 - 384 = \boxed{}$

Number pairs

How much more to reach the target?

1. £3500 + £500 = £4000

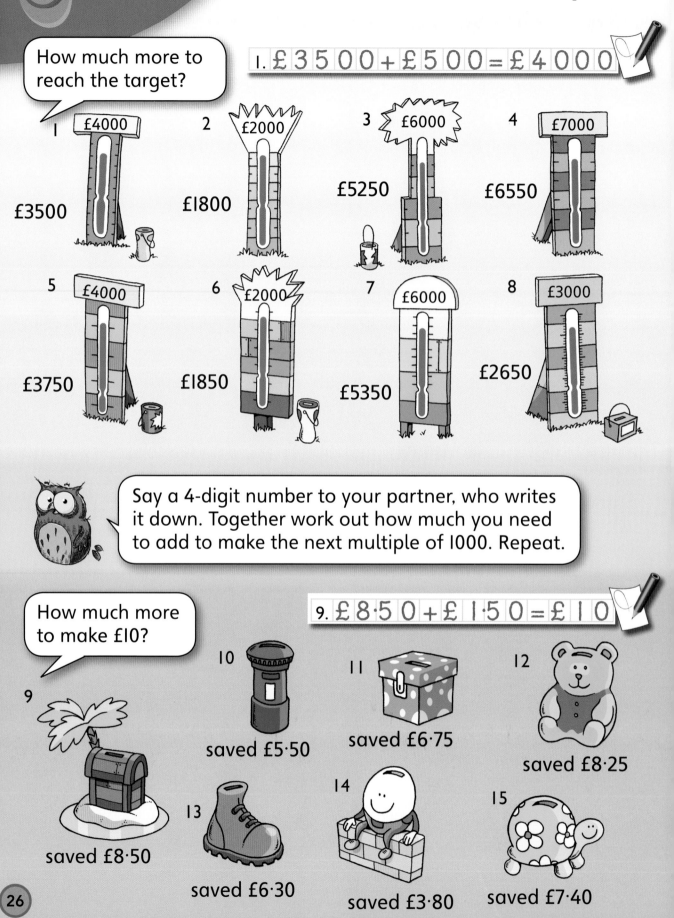

1   £4000   £3500

2   £2000   £1800

3   £6000   £5250

4   £7000   £6550

5   £4000   £3750

6   £2000   £1850

7   £6000   £5350

8   £3000   £2650

Say a 4-digit number to your partner, who writes it down. Together work out how much you need to add to make the next multiple of 1000. Repeat.

How much more to make £10?

9. £8·50 + £1·50 = £10

9   saved £8·50

10   saved £5·50

11   saved £6·75

12   saved £8·25

13   saved £6·30

14   saved £3·80

15   saved £7·40

2D shapes

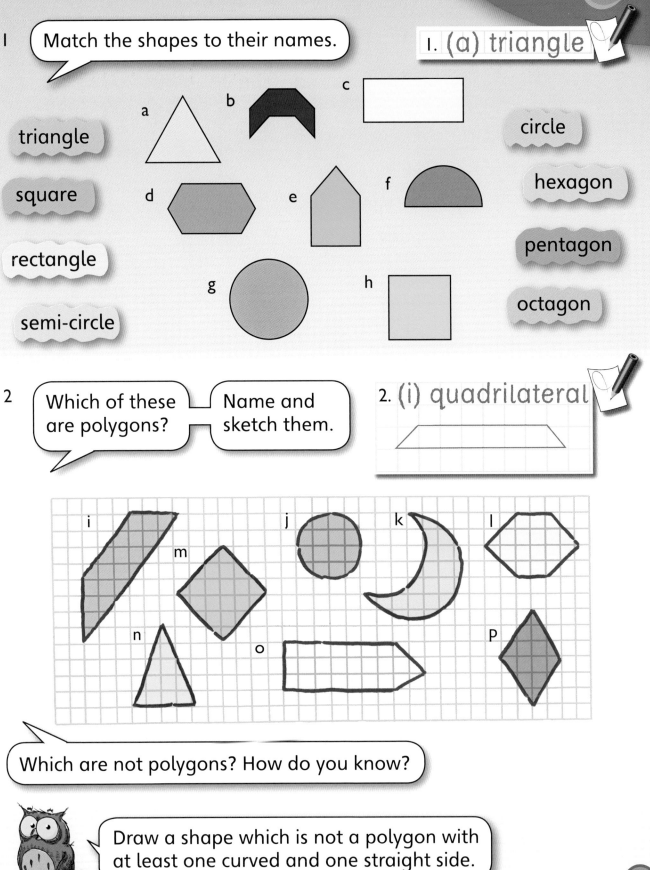

l Match the shapes to their names.

1. (a) triangle

triangle

square

rectangle

semi-circle

circle

hexagon

pentagon

octagon

2 Which of these are polygons? Name and sketch them.

2. (i) quadrilateral

Which are not polygons? How do you know?

Draw a shape which is not a polygon with at least one curved and one straight side.

27

2D shapes

Name the polygons in the picture.

1.

1. (a) triangle

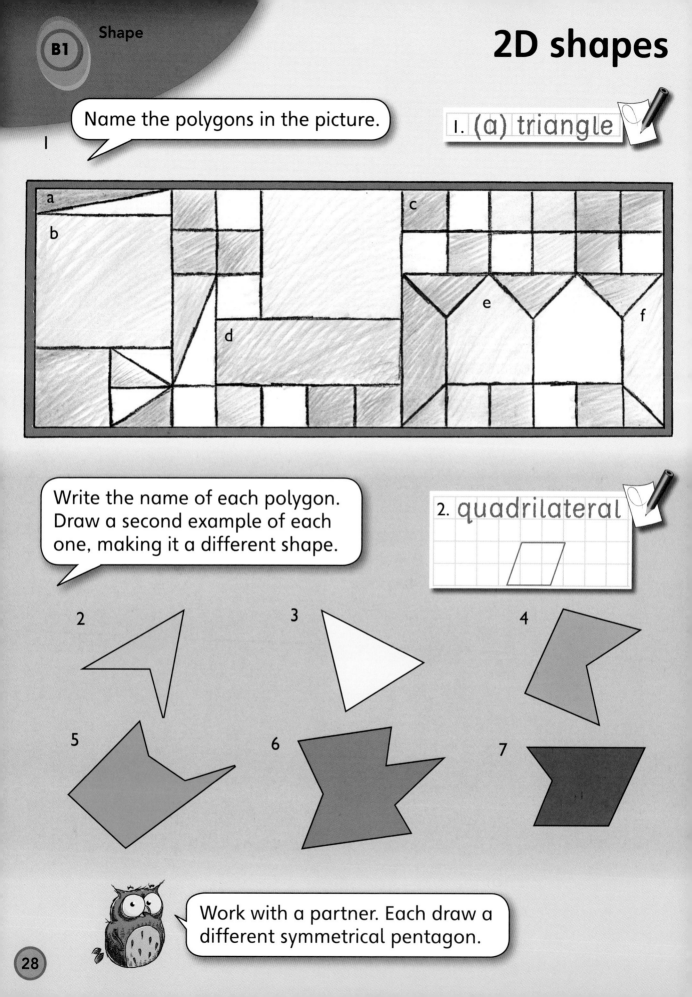

Write the name of each polygon. Draw a second example of each one, making it a different shape.

2. quadrilateral

2

3

4

5

6

7

Work with a partner. Each draw a different symmetrical pentagon.

2D shapes

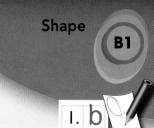

Which of the shapes below are:

| 1 | squares | 2 | rectangles | 3 | triangles |
| 4 | pentagons | 5 | hexagons | 6 | quadrilaterals |

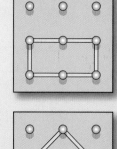

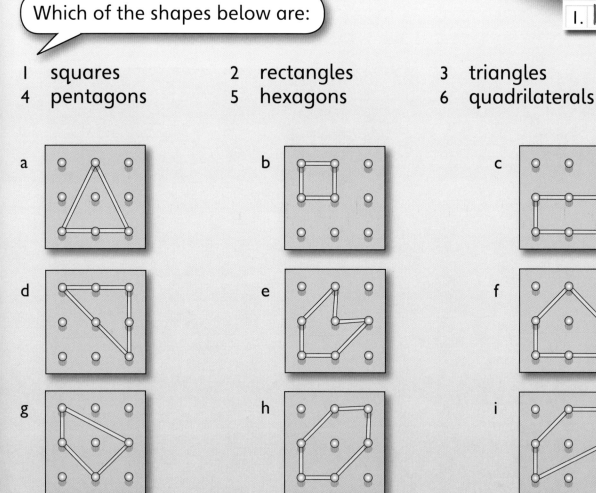

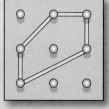

Explore

Start with a triangle.

Add another triangle.

Keep adding triangles.

Write the name of each shape you make as you go.

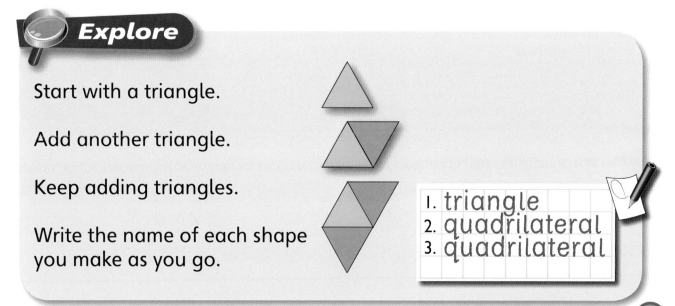

1. triangle
2. quadrilateral
3. quadrilateral

Polygons

Name each polygon. Circle the regular ones.

1. triangle

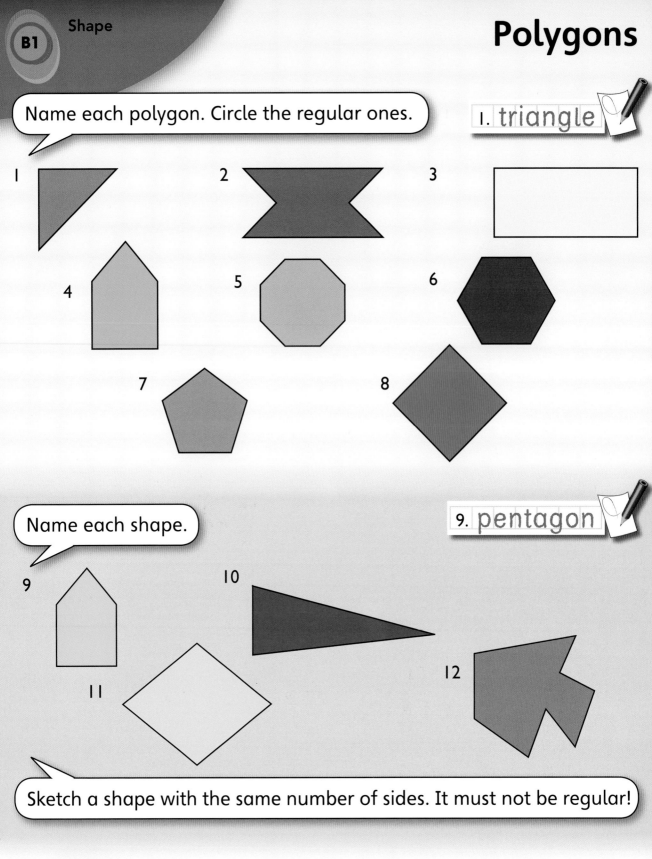

Name each shape.

9. pentagon

Sketch a shape with the same number of sides. It must not be regular!

How many quadrilaterals can you sketch? They must all be different and they must not be regular.

Triangles

1

Which are equilateral triangles?
Which are isosceles triangles?

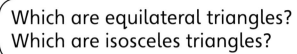
1. a, ...

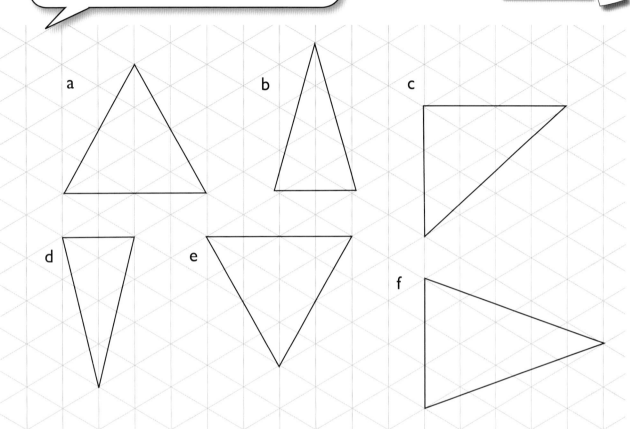

2

Look at the triangles below. Use dotted paper to draw other triangles on 3 × 3 grids. How many more can you find? Can you name any?

Triangles

1 For each triangle, say whether it is equilateral, isosceles or scalene.

1. (a) equilateral

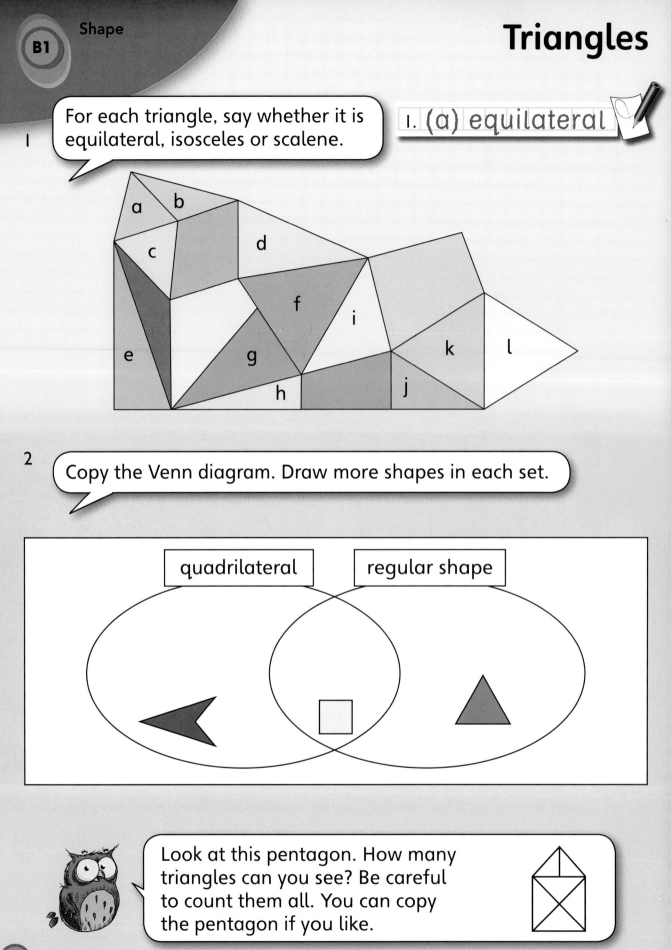

2 Copy the Venn diagram. Draw more shapes in each set.

quadrilateral   regular shape

Look at this pentagon. How many triangles can you see? Be careful to count them all. You can copy the pentagon if you like.

Triangles

1. f

Match the clues to the shapes.

1 It has five sides, none of them equal.

a

f   d

2 It looks like two triangles stuck together.

3 It looks like half a regular hexagon.

c

b

4 It has one more side than an octagon.

5 It has three sides and is not regular.

e

g

6 It has half the number of sides of an octagon.

Draw some shapes. Make up your own clues for your partner to work out.

Explore

Draw round a regular hexagon. Join different corners with straight lines. What different shapes can you make?

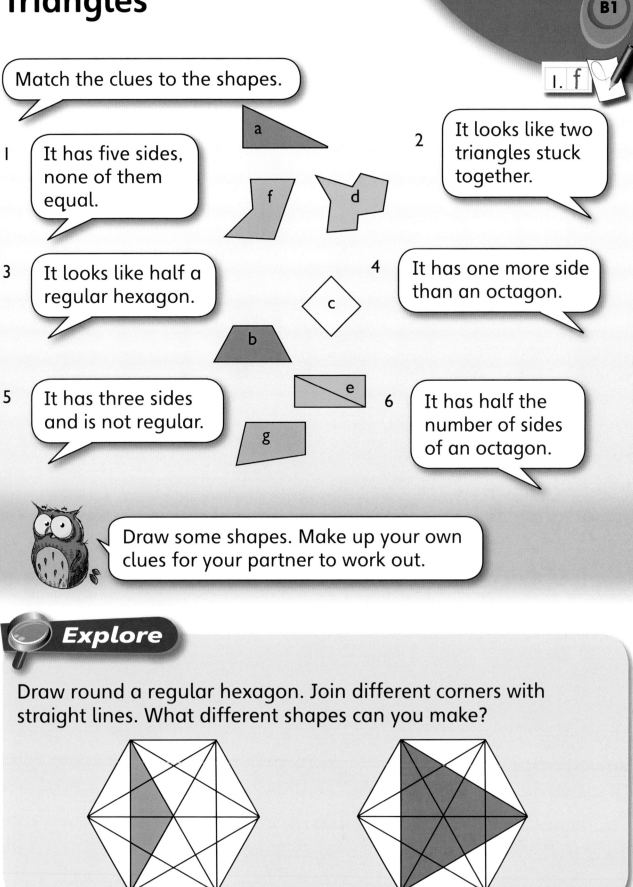

Centimetres and metres

Measure each millipede using a ruler. Write the number of centimetres.

1. 8 c m

1

2

3

4

5

6

Write the number of centimetres.

7. $1\frac{1}{2}$ m = 1 5 0 c m

7　$1\frac{1}{2}$ m

8　$1\frac{1}{4}$ m

9　2 m

10　$1\frac{3}{4}$ m

11　$\frac{1}{2}$ m

12　$2\frac{1}{4}$ m

Look around the classroom. Write a list of things that are between $\frac{1}{2}$ m and 1 m long.

Centimetres and metres

Look at each space object in the picture. Write its measurements in metres and centimetres.

1. $1.5 m = 150 cm$

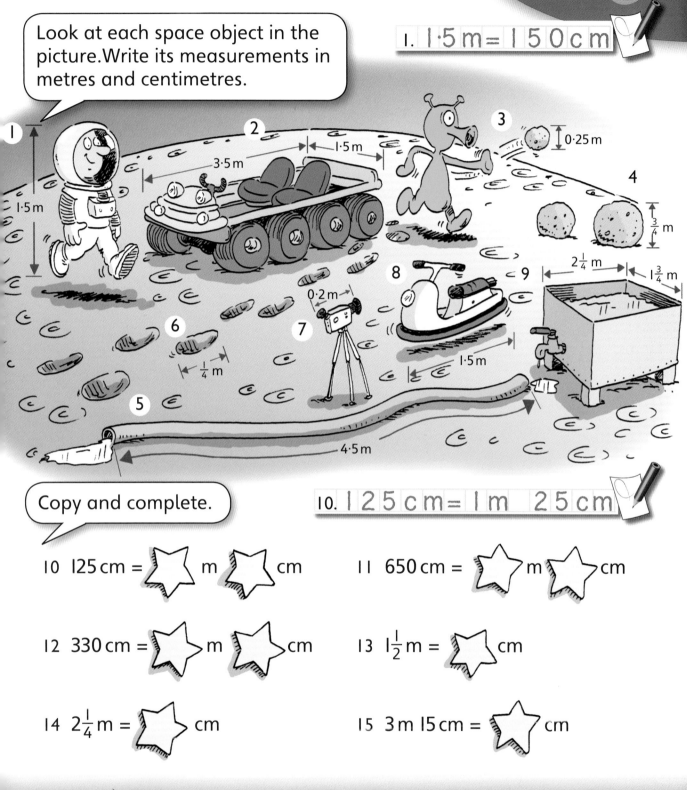

Copy and complete.

10. $125 cm = 1 m \quad 25 cm$

10 $125 cm = \bigstar m \bigstar cm$

11 $650 cm = \bigstar m \bigstar cm$

12 $330 cm = \bigstar m \bigstar cm$

13 $1\frac{1}{2} m = \bigstar cm$

14 $2\frac{1}{4} m = \bigstar cm$

15 $3 m \ 15 cm = \bigstar cm$

Work with a partner. Measure your longest and shortest fingers in centimetres.

Millimetres

Use a ruler to measure the length of each leaf in centimetres and millimetres.

1. 7 c m   8 mm

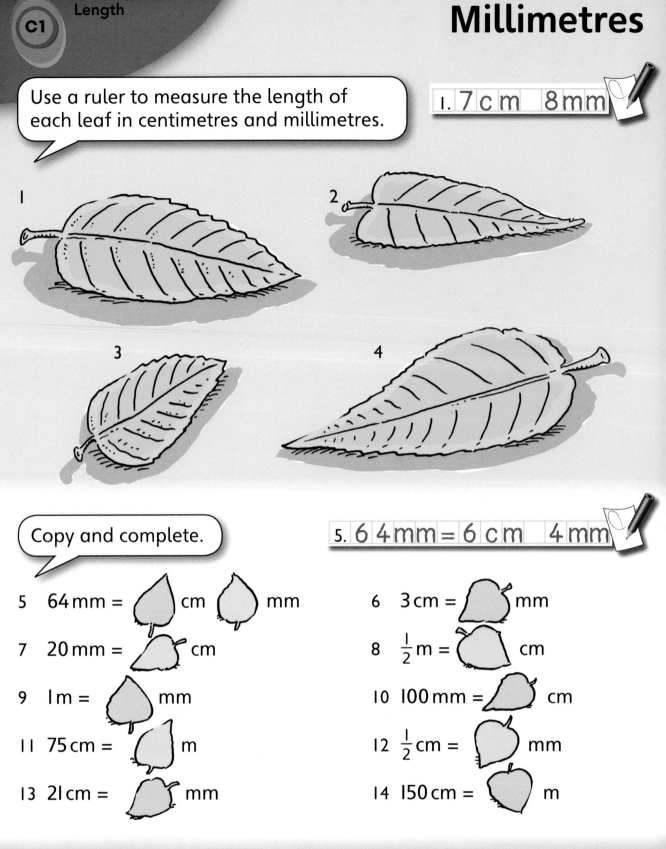

Copy and complete.

5. 6 4 mm = 6 c m   4 mm

5 64 mm = ◯ cm ◯ mm

6 3 cm = ◯ mm

7 20 mm = ◯ cm

8 $\frac{1}{2}$ m = ◯ cm

9 1 m = ◯ mm

10 100 mm = ◯ cm

11 75 cm = ◯ m

12 $\frac{1}{2}$ cm = ◯ mm

13 21 cm = ◯ mm

14 150 cm = ◯ m

Measure your pencil in millimetres.
Sharpen it. What does it measure now?

Millimetres, centimetres and metres

1 Write each distance in metres.

1. a to b: 1000m

I need to visit every village, flying along the paths. What is the shortest route? How many metres will I have to fly in total?

2 Choose an object in the picture. Write what unit you would use to measure it. Repeat ten times.

2. House: metres

Millimetres, centimetres and metres

Write each ribbon length in centimetres.

If each ribbon were ten times longer, how long would it be in metres?

1. 35 cm
   350 cm = 3 m 50 cm

1 350 mm

2 460 mm

3 210 mm

4 100 mm

5 340 mm

6 990 mm

Miles are longer than kilometres:
3 miles is about 5 km.
Rewrite each sign in kilometres.

7. 3 miles = 5 km

7 Splashville 3 miles

8 Wettown 6 miles

9 Mudvillage 30 miles

10 Swampston 9 miles

11 Little Dripston 60 miles

12 Rainscombe 12 miles

13 Kareena buys $1\frac{1}{2}$ m of ribbon. She cuts off 60 cm. How much does she have left?

14 You have 6 presents. You need 25 cm of string to wrap each present. The string costs 10p per metre. How much will you spend?

Area

Write the area of each shape in squares.

1. area = 5 squares

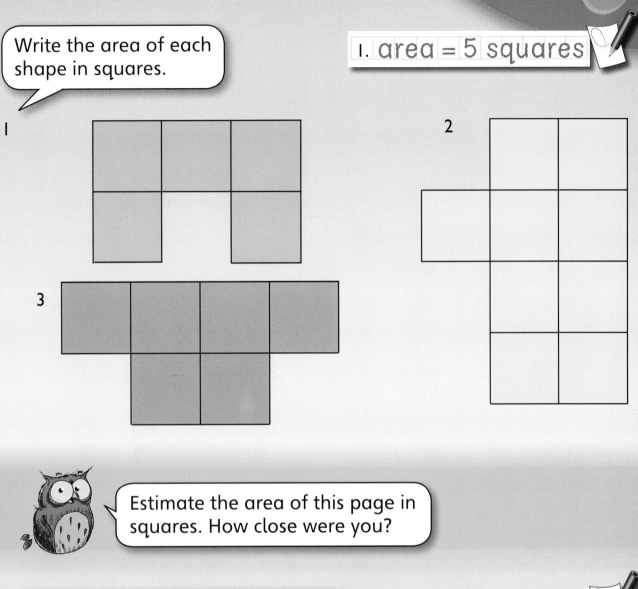

1

2

3

Estimate the area of this page in squares. How close were you?

Write the area of tiles on each floor.

4. area = 14 tiles

4

5

6

Draw four more small rooms with tiles.

Write the area of each stain. Only count part squares if they are half a square or more.

1. 5 squares

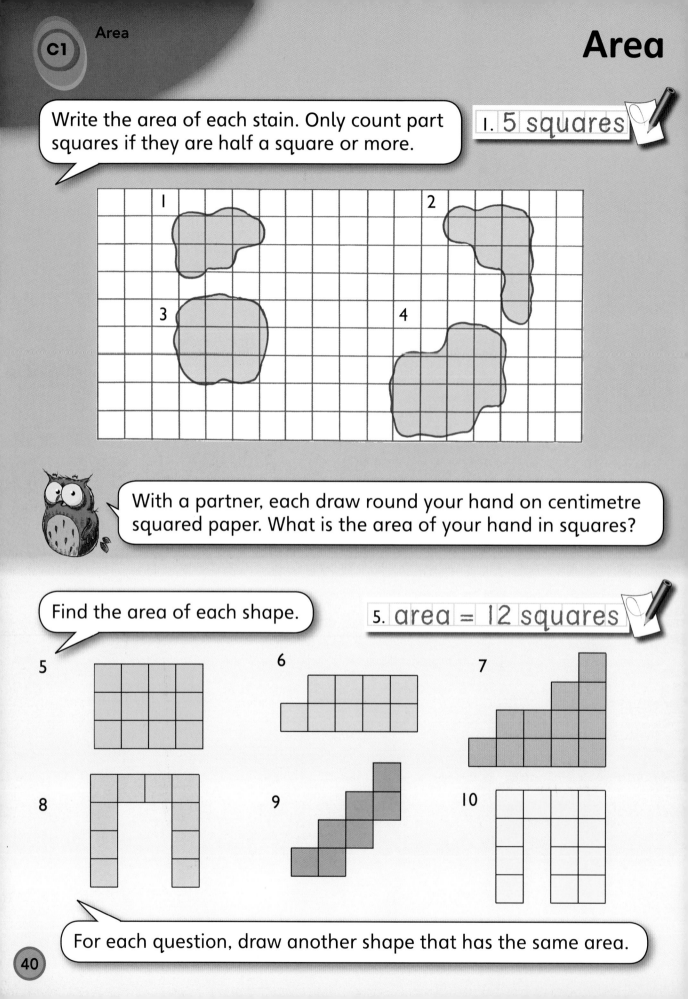

1

2

3

4

With a partner, each draw round your hand on centimetre squared paper. What is the area of your hand in squares?

Find the area of each shape.

5. area = 12 squares

5

6

7

8

9

10

For each question, draw another shape that has the same area.

Area

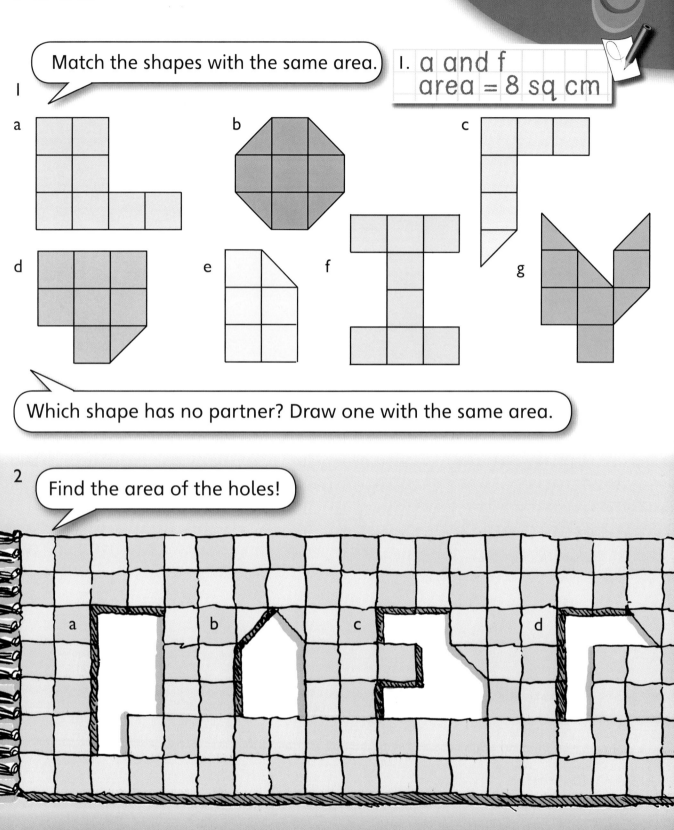

Match the shapes with the same area.

1. a and f
   area = 8 sq cm

1

a   b   c

d   e   f   g

Which shape has no partner? Draw one with the same area.

2

Find the area of the holes!

a   b   c   d

On cm squared paper, how many different shapes
can you draw that have an area of 6 square cm?

Tally charts and frequency tables

Draw frequency tables to match each of these two tally charts.

I. Class pets

Pets	Frequency
Cat	13

1

Class pets

Pets	Tallies
Cat	卌 卌 |||
Dog	卌 卌 卌	
Rabbit	卌 ||
Hamster	卌 ||||

2

Survey of favourite animals

Animal	Tallies
Chimpanzee	卌 卌 卌 ||
Lion	卌 卌 ||
Giraffe	卌 卌 卌 卌 卌	
Shark	卌 卌 卌 卌	
Horse	卌 卌 卌 卌 卌 卌 |||

Which of the four pets was:

3   the most common

4   the least common

Which of the five animals was:

5   the favourite

6   the second favourite

7   the least favourite

8   How many pets in the class altogether?

9   What was the total number of animal votes?

10   Are there other pets you might include in the pet tally chart?

11   What might be different if this was your class:
    a   about the numbers
    b   about the animals shown?

Talk with a friend about other things you could make a frequency table for.

Frequency tables

The table shows how many times these animals were seen one day on a camping holiday.

Animals seen	
Animal	**Frequency**
Fox	3
Squirrel	12
Hedgehog	2
Duck	16
Rabbit	8
Horse	7
Cow	23

Which of the animals was seen:

1 most frequently

2 least frequently

Which animal was seen: 3 8 times 4 7 times 5 12 times?

Which animals were seen:

6 more than 10 times   7 fewer than 8 times?

8 Which animal was seen twice as many times as a rabbit?

9 How many animals were seen altogether?

If you were camping by the sea or in a forest, what different animals might you see?
Think of other places you could camp.
Draw up a frequency table for one of them.

Frequency tables

The picture shows the four types of minibeast found in a flower bed.

1 Count how many of each, then draw a frequency table to show the totals.

1. Animal	Frequency
ant	
woodlouse	
ladybird	
spider	

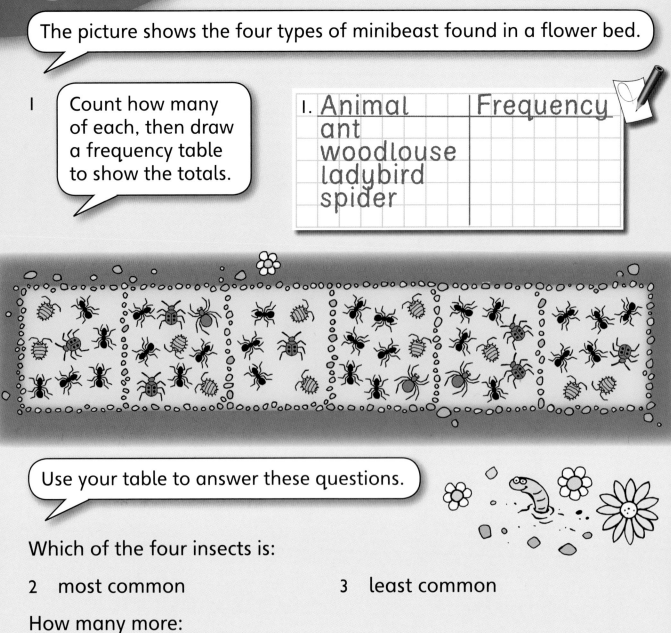

Use your table to answer these questions.

Which of the four insects is:

2 most common

3 least common

How many more:

4 ants than spiders

5 woodlice than ladybirds

6 ladybirds than spiders

7 ants than woodlice?

8 How many insects altogether?

Draw a picture to show which part of the flower bed has the most of each insect.

Frequency tables

Here are the names of different breeds of dog.

Bulldog
Dalmatian
Beagle
Bloodhound
Greyhound
Wolfhound
Collie
Alsatian
Terrier
Labrador
Spaniel
Pekingese
Poodle
Red Setter
Dachshund
Saint Bernard
Whippet
Great Dane

Vowel	Frequency
a	
e	
i	
o	
u	

Draw a frequency table to show how often each vowel appears.

Write about the information in the table.

Find out which consonants appear most often.

Pictograms

The pictogram shows the number of days each bird was spotted in I month.

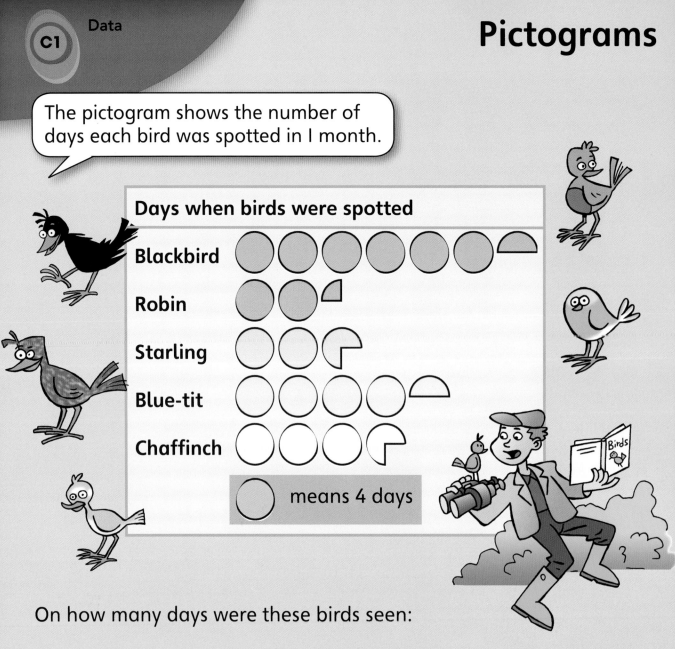

Days when birds were spotted

Blackbird	
Robin	
Starling	
Blue-tit	
Chaffinch	

○ means 4 days

On how many days were these birds seen:

I   starlings   2   chaffinches   3   robins   4   blackbirds?

Which type of bird was seen:

5   most often   6   least often?

7   Which type of bird was seen half as often as the blue-tit?

If the month was July, on how many days was each bird not spotted?

Pictograms

Draw a pictogram to show how many butterflies of each colour can be seen. Use 🦋 to show two butterflies.

How many of the butterflies are:

1 white   2 red   3 yellow   4 blue?

How many more are:

5 yellow than blue   6 white than red?

7 Which colour butterfly was seen half as often as the yellow?

Ask your partner questions about the pictogram. Write down three questions and their answers.

Pictograms

The pictogram shows the number of eggs laid by the hens in I week.

Eggs laid

Monday	
Tuesday	
Wednesday	
Thursday	
Friday	
Saturday	
Sunday	

means 6 eggs

Write how many eggs were collected on:

1 Wednesday   2 Friday   3 the weekend   4 weekdays

On which two consecutive days were:

5 25 eggs collected   6 30 eggs collected

7 How many egg boxes are needed to pack the eggs for the week?

 **Explore**

If eggs were boxed in 4s, what symbol would you use to represent the data? Redraw the pictogram to show this.

Design a pictogram to show how much milk was collected from a farm each day.

Adding several numbers

Add the scores.

Look for pairs to 10.

1. $4 + 6 + 5 = 15$

1. 5 6 4
2. 7 8 3
3. 6 4 6
4. 8 7 2
5. 9 3 7
6. 5 6 5

Using three single-digit numbers, how many different ways can you make 15?

$\square + \square + \square = 15$

What is each player's total score?

Add the 9 last.

7. $5 + 8 = 13$
$13 + 9 = 22$

7. 5 8 9
8. 4 9 5
9. 3 9 8
10. 9 4 7

11. 6 9 8
12. 7 7 9
13. 9 8 8
14. 6 9 5

15. 8 12 9
16. 4 3 9 6
17. 7 4 3 9
18. 13 8 9

Adding several numbers

Find the total time for each child's tasks.

1. $8 + 2 + 5 + 3 = 18$ minutes
    _10_/

Look for pairs to 10.

1
Clear table:
3 minutes
Wash up:
8 minutes
Dry up:
5 minutes
Put cutlery away: 2 minutes

2
Feed dog: 6 minutes
Let dog out: 7 minutes
Tidy up dog bowls:
4 minutes
Brush dog:
8 minutes

3
Find school bag: 5 minutes
Do homework: 9 minutes
Find gym kit:
5 minutes
Pack gym bag:
6 minutes
Make sandwiches: 9 minutes

4
Make bed: 3 minutes
Tidy toys: 3 minutes
Dust shelves: 4 minutes
Clean shoes: 9 minutes
Put away clothes:
7 minutes

Write three numbers between 2 and 10. Your partner does the same. Both guess the answer if you add all six numbers. Both do the addition. Who was closest?

Add the card numbers.

5. $30 + 70 + 80 + 40 = 220$

Look for pairs to 100.

5 | 40 | 70 | 80 | 30 |

6 | 50 | 60 | 50 | 80 |

7 | 60 | 70 | 70 | 40 |

8 | 80 | 70 | 40 | 20 | 30 |

9 | 70 | 10 | 90 | 90 |

10 | 70 | 60 | 90 | 30 |

11 | 80 | 60 | 90 | 20 |

12 | 60 | 80 | 50 | 40 |

Adding several numbers

How long was each firework display?

1. $8 + 2 + 6 + 3 = 19$ minutes

1
3 minutes
8 minutes
6 minutes
2 minutes

2
6 minutes
3 minutes
3 minutes
7 minutes
8 minutes

3
5 minutes
7 minutes
9 minutes
8 minutes
5 minutes

4
8 minutes
5 minutes
3 minutes
7 minutes

5
4 minutes
5 minutes
6 minutes
3 minutes
8 minutes

Choose one of the additions above. Add the numbers in a different order. Do you get the same answer? What happens if you take one of the numbers away? Does the order matter then? Look at my example: $8 + 6 + 3 - 2$ $6 - 2 + 8 + 3$

6 Choose five card numbers.   Add them.   Repeat six times.

Look for pairs to 100.

6. $40 + 60 + 80 + 20 + 90 = 290$

90   20   40   80   70   80   50   70   30   60   90

Adding several numbers

Copy and complete.

1. $9 + 8 + 2 + 3 = 25 - 3$

1   $9 + 8 + \boxed{} + 3 = 25 - 3$

2   $7 + 6 + \boxed{} + 4 + 9 = 33 - 1$

3   $6 + 8 + \boxed{} + 9 = 25 + 4$

4   $14 + 8 + 6 + \boxed{} = 33 + 4$

5   $13 + 9 + 8 + \boxed{} = 40 - 3$

6   $7 + 7 + \boxed{} + 8 = 40 - 10$

7   $6 + 7 + 4 + \boxed{} = 33 - 4$

8   $7 + 8 + \boxed{} + 9 = 31 - 2$

9   $15 + 8 + 6 + 9 + \boxed{} = 45 + 1$

10   $11 + 6 + \boxed{} + 9 = 29 + 4$

Explore

We know that: $480 + 370 + 560 + 90 = 1500$
and that: $240 + 680 + 750 = 1670$

Which of the following calculations do we know are correct without doing much work? Are any incorrect?

a $240 + 750 = 990$

b $370 + 560 + 90 = 1020$

c $480 + 370 + 560 = 1410$

d $1500 - 560 = 480 + 370 + 90$

e $480 + 370 + 90 = 940$

f $990 + 680 = 1670$

Use a calculator to write and complete a complicated addition. Now write some other calculations which become easy if you use your addition.

Adding and subtracting multiples of 10

Copy and complete.

1. $14 - 6 = 8$
   $140 - 60 = 80$

1 $14 - 6 = \boxed{}$

   $140 - 60 = \boxed{}$

2 $17 + 5 = \boxed{}$

   $170 + 50 = \boxed{}$

3 $16 - 7 = \boxed{}$

   $160 - 70 = \boxed{}$

4 $24 + 8 = \boxed{}$

   $240 + 80 = \boxed{}$

5 $12 - 5 = \boxed{}$

   $120 - 50 = \boxed{}$

6 $17 + 9 = \boxed{}$

   $170 + 90 = \boxed{}$

7 $18 + 7 = \boxed{}$

   $180 + 70 = \boxed{}$

8 $13 - 7 = \boxed{}$

   $130 - 70 = \boxed{}$

9 $15 - 8 = \boxed{}$

   $150 - 80 = \boxed{}$

10 $23 - 9 = \boxed{}$

    $230 - 90 = \boxed{}$

11 $21 - 8 = \boxed{}$

    $210 - 80 = \boxed{}$

12 $11 - 7 = \boxed{}$

    $110 - 70 = \boxed{}$

13 Choose one red card and one yellow card. — Find the total and the difference. — Do this six times.

150   50   90   510   60

320   240   70   120

Try adding all the red cards, then adding all the yellow cards, and finding the difference between the two totals.

Adding and subtracting multiples of 10

Find the total crowd at each concert. Find the difference between the numbers of adults and children.

1. $310 - 70 = 240$

1 310 adults, 70 children

2 220 adults, 70 children

3 440 adults, 80 children

4 230 adults, 90 children

5 340 adults, 60 children

6 150 adults, 80 children

7 210 adults, 80 children

Tickets cost £10 for adults and £5 for children. How much does each concert make?

Copy and complete.

8. $320 - 60 = 260$

8 $320 - 60 = \boxed{}$

9 $430 - 80 = \boxed{}$

10 $370 + 70 = \boxed{}$

11 $360 + 80 = \boxed{}$

12 $880 + 40 = \boxed{}$

13 $830 - 60 = \boxed{}$

14 $710 - 90 = \boxed{}$

15 $280 + 50 = \boxed{}$

16 $640 + 50 = \boxed{}$

Adding and subtracting multiples of 10

Copy and complete.

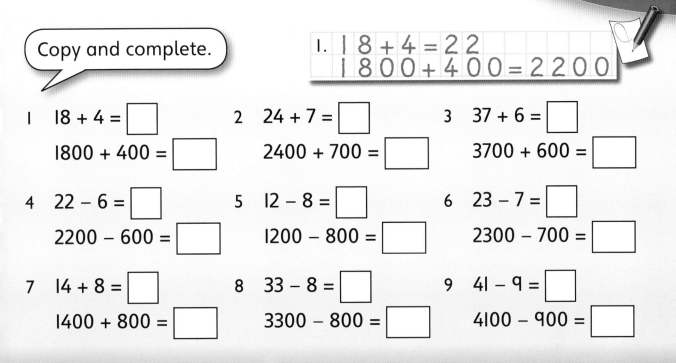

1. $18 + 4 = 22$
   $1800 + 400 = 2200$

1 $18 + 4 = \boxed{}$

$1800 + 400 = \boxed{}$

2 $24 + 7 = \boxed{}$

$2400 + 700 = \boxed{}$

3 $37 + 6 = \boxed{}$

$3700 + 600 = \boxed{}$

4 $22 - 6 = \boxed{}$

$2200 - 600 = \boxed{}$

5 $12 - 8 = \boxed{}$

$1200 - 800 = \boxed{}$

6 $23 - 7 = \boxed{}$

$2300 - 700 = \boxed{}$

7 $14 + 8 = \boxed{}$

$1400 + 800 = \boxed{}$

8 $33 - 8 = \boxed{}$

$3300 - 800 = \boxed{}$

9 $41 - 9 = \boxed{}$

$4100 - 900 = \boxed{}$

Imagine that you and your partner each have a fistful of £10 notes. The difference is £90. The total is less than £400. How many £10 notes might you each have?

10 Jane has saved £210 and Afram has saved £390. Find the total amount saved. How much more does Afram have than Jane?

11 Ian runs 480 m in his first race and 260 m in his second race. How much longer was the first race and how far did he run in total?

12 A plane flies 3200 miles to London and 2400 miles to Athens. How far does it fly in total? What is the difference between the two distances?

Adding and subtracting multiples of 10

Copy and complete.

1. 1800 + 600 = 2400

1   1800 + 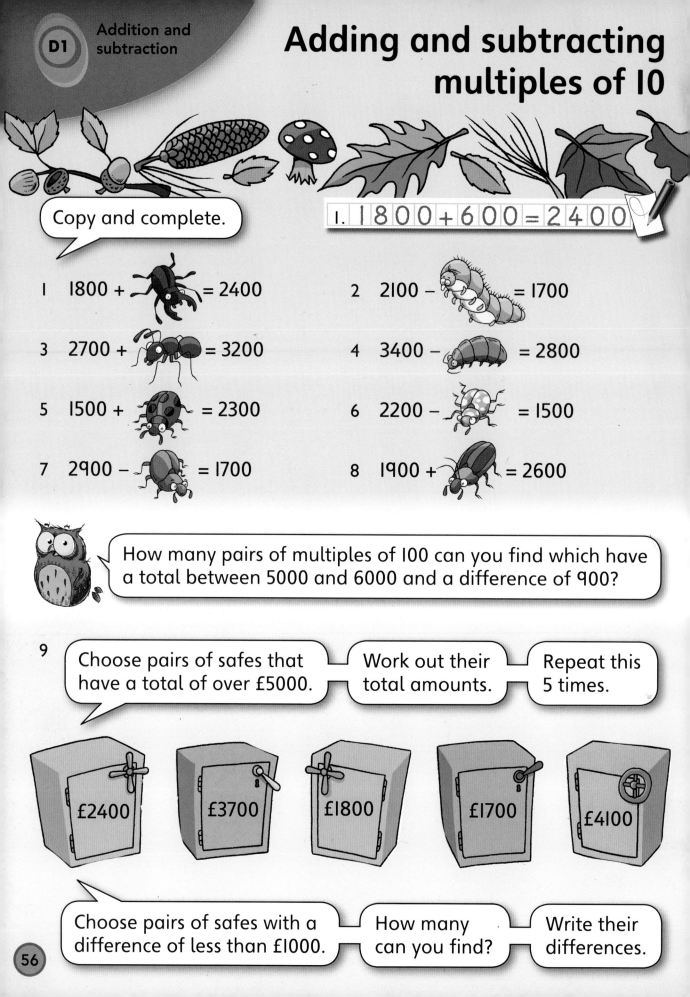 = 2400

2   2100 – 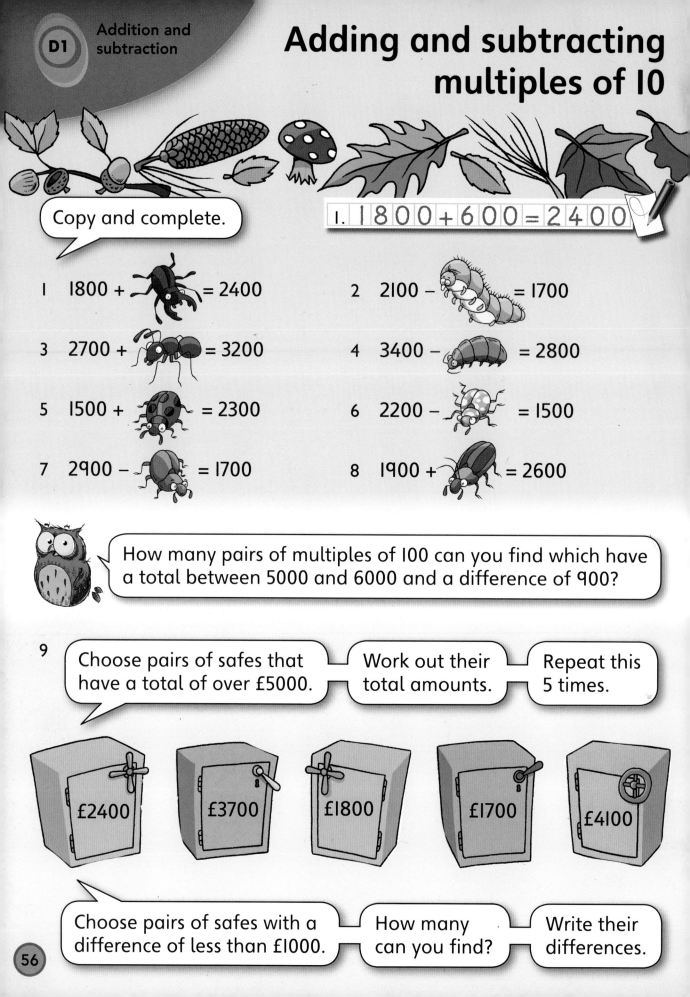 = 1700

3   2700 + 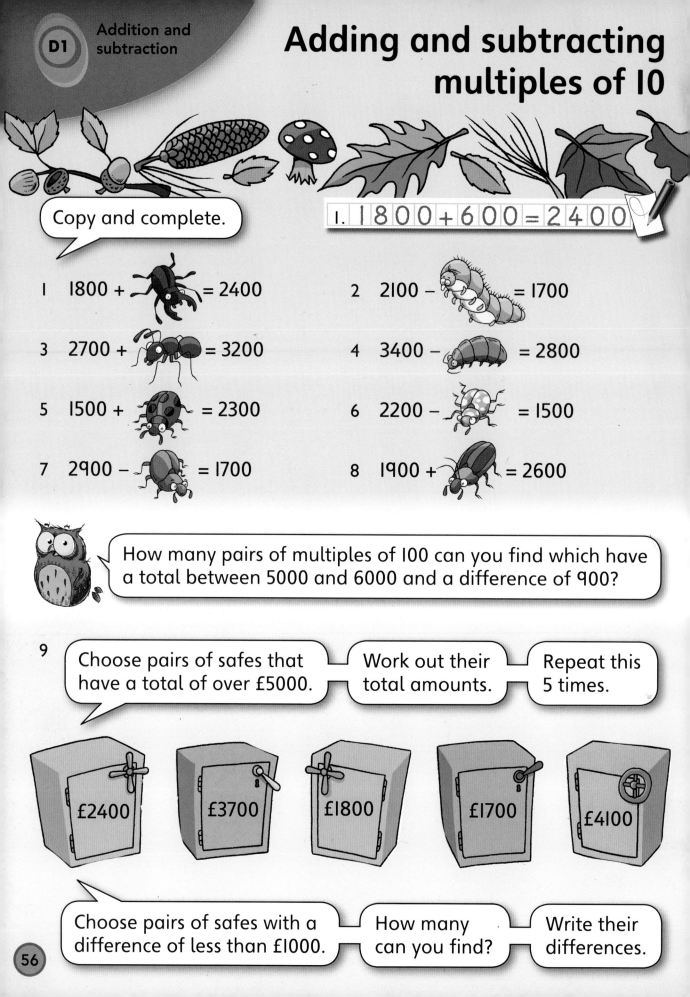 = 3200

4   3400 – 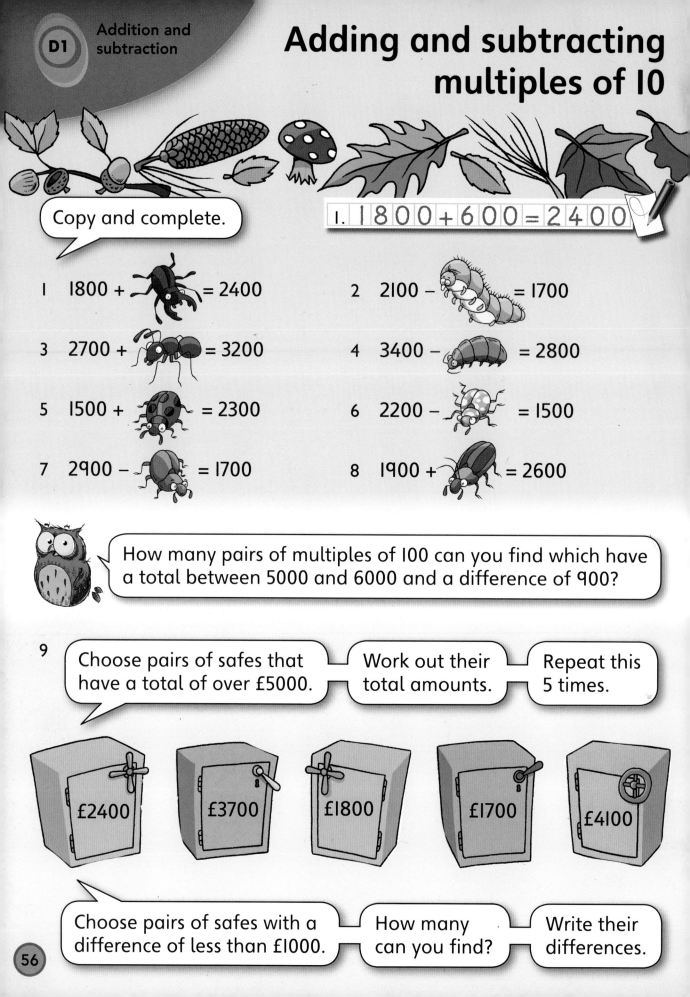 = 2800

5   1500 + 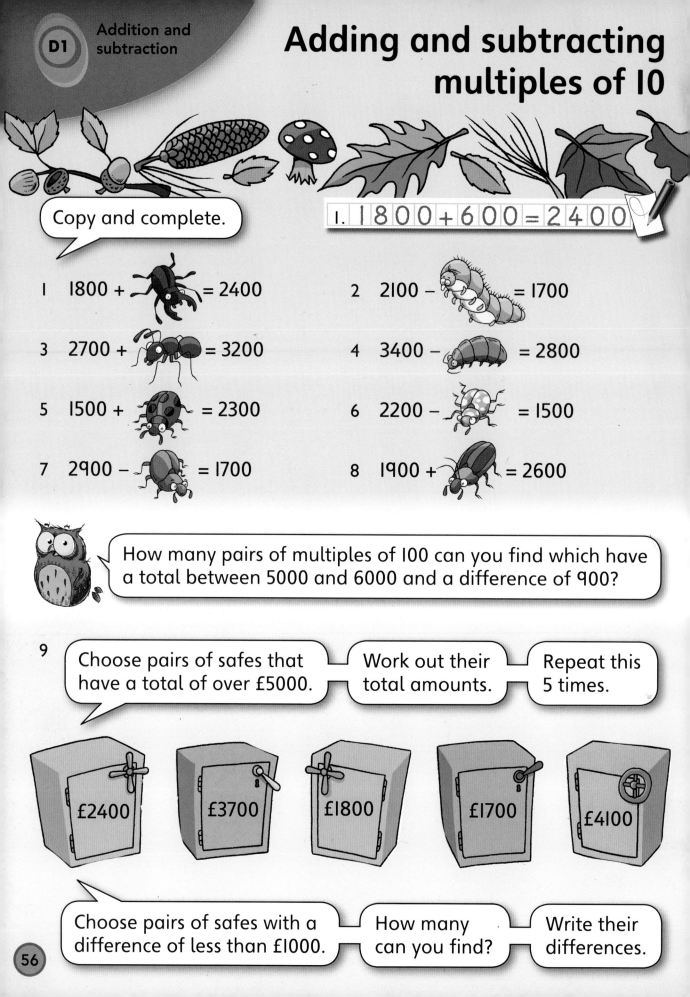 = 2300

6   2200 – 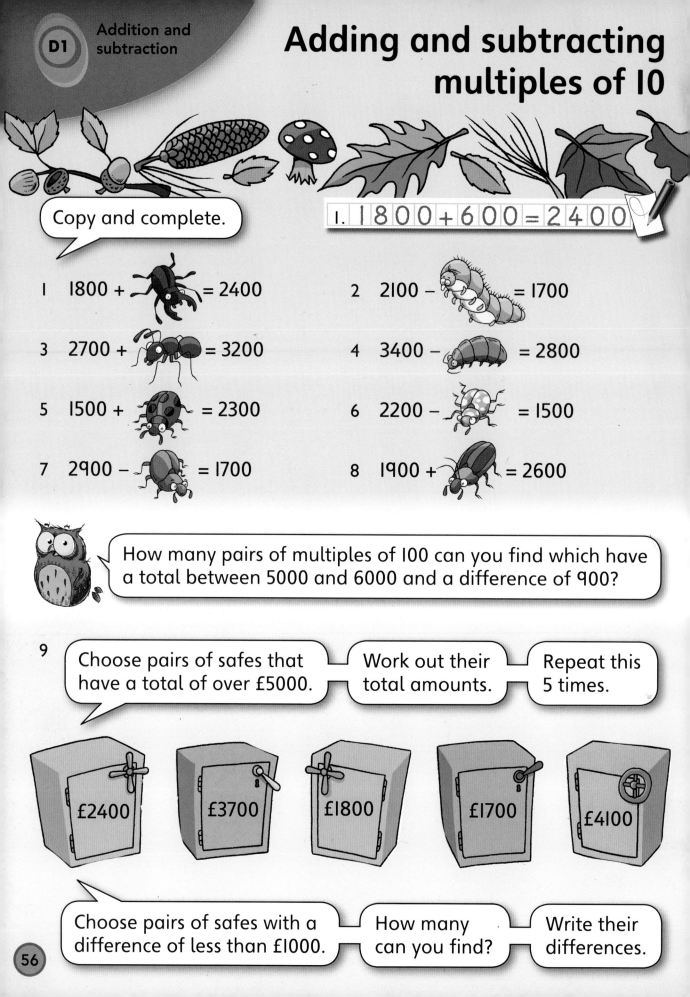 = 1500

7   2900 – 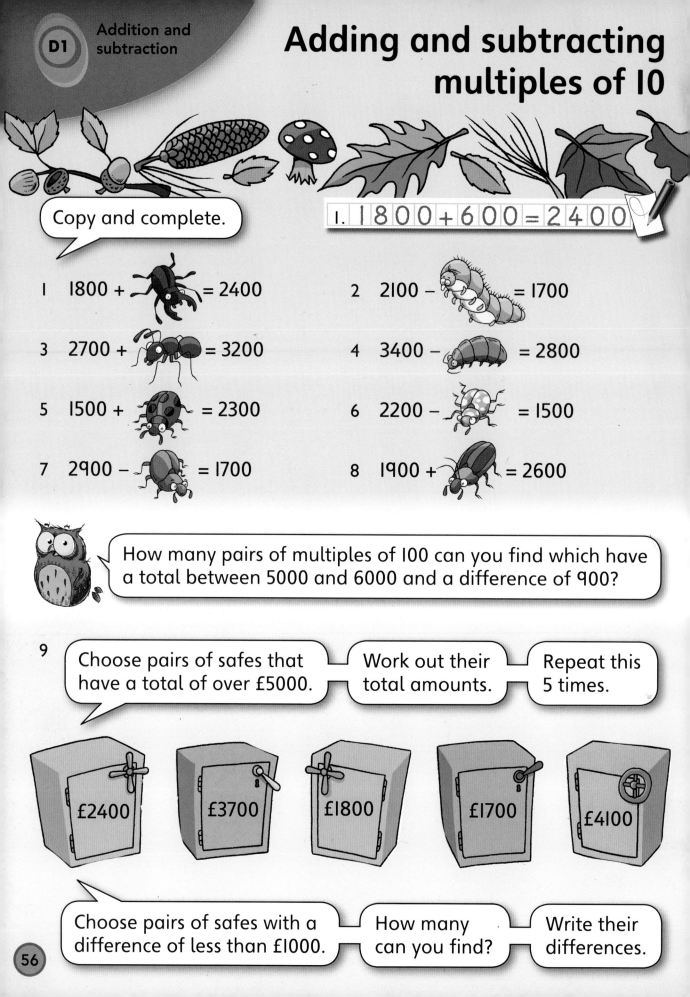 = 1700

8   1900 + 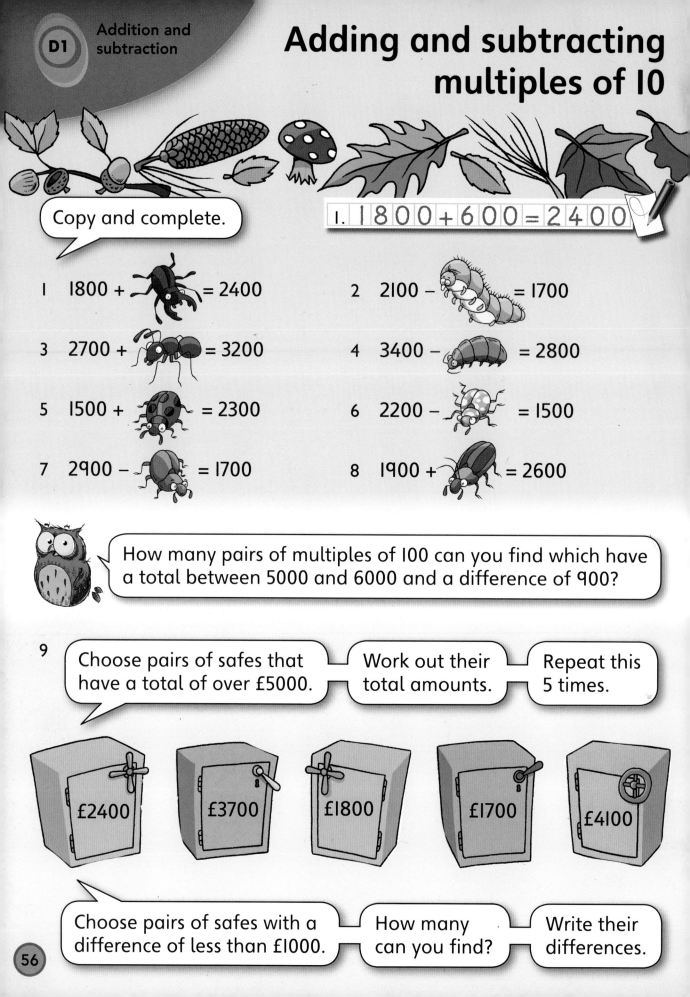 = 2600

How many pairs of multiples of 100 can you find which have a total between 5000 and 6000 and a difference of 900?

9   Choose pairs of safes that have a total of over £5000. — Work out their total amounts. — Repeat this 5 times.

£2400   £3700   £1800   £1700   £4100

Choose pairs of safes with a difference of less than £1000. — How many can you find? — Write their differences.

Write the number of minutes past each hour.

1. 21

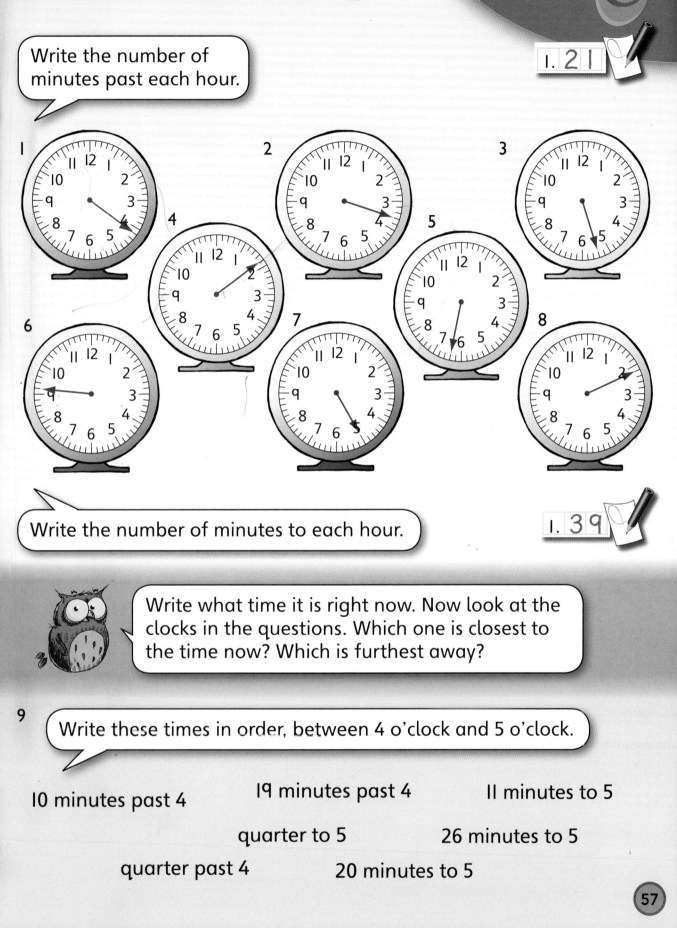

Write the number of minutes to each hour.

1. 39

Write what time it is right now. Now look at the clocks in the questions. Which one is closest to the time now? Which is furthest away?

9

Write these times in order, between 4 o'clock and 5 o'clock.

10 minutes past 4   19 minutes past 4   11 minutes to 5

quarter to 5   26 minutes to 5

quarter past 4   20 minutes to 5

Reading the time

Write the time on each clock using 'past' or 'to'.

1. 27 minutes past 2

Write the digital time to match each clock.

1. 2:27

Write these digital times:

6. 7:55

6 10 minutes later than

7:45

7 10 minutes earlier than

8:14

8 20 minutes later than

9:52

9 20 minutes earlier than

6:15

10 25 minutes earlier than

10:55

11 15 minutes earlier than

4:07

 Write the time you wake up. Write the time you go to sleep. How long are you awake for? How long are you asleep for?

Reading the time

Write the time on each clock using 'past' or 'to'.

1. 11 minutes past 3

1 3:11

2 4:26

3 1:35

4 2:50

5 3:37

6 6:43

7 9:18

8 12:32

9 7:46

Write the times in order, starting at 1:35. Find the time gap between each.

Write the missing time in each sequence.

10. 6:15 pm

10 5:45 pm, 6:00 pm, [   ] , 6:30 pm

11 3:38 am, 3:48 am, 3:58 am, [   ]

12 10:45 pm, 11:45 pm, [   ] , 1:45 am

13 9:16 am, 10.16 am, 11:16 am, [   ]

14 9:48 am, 11:48 am, [   ] , 3:48 pm

15 6:25 pm, 8:25 pm, 10:25 pm, [   ]

am and pm

Write each time using am or pm.

I. 7:20 am

1

2

3

4

5

6

7 Jon wakes up at 7:45 am. He takes 12 minutes to wash and get dressed, 16 minutes over breakfast, then leaves for school. It takes him 9 minutes to walk to school. What time does he arrive?

8 Kareena sets off to meet Kim at a train station. She catches the 8:25 am train and the journey takes 2 hours 11 minutes. Kim catches the 9:16 am train and her journey lasts 1 hour 50 minutes. Who gets there first, and how long does she have to wait?

Write the time half way between each pair of clock times:

9 8:52   9:24

10 10:16   2:40

11 3:48   4:20

12 7:50   8:36

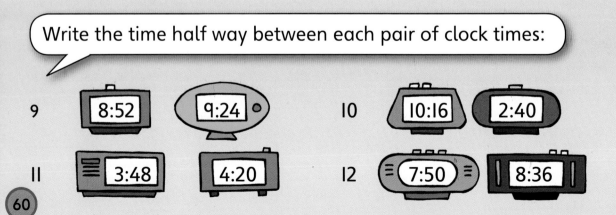

Seconds

Write how many seconds have passed after the minute.

1. 17 seconds

1

2

3

4

5

6

Write how many seconds to the next minute.

1. 43 seconds

Write how many seconds in:

7. 60 seconds

7 (1 minute) 8 ($\frac{1}{2}$ minute) 9 (2 minutes)

10 (5 minutes) 11 (10 minutes) 12 ($\frac{1}{4}$ of a minute)

I bounce a ball every second for $5\frac{1}{2}$ minutes. How many times does it bounce in total?

The children in Class 4 ran an obstacle race. These are their times.

Gita
2 minutes
18 seconds

Jenny
1 minute
54 seconds

Anna
2 minutes
38 seconds

Afram
3 minutes
11 seconds

Lisa
1 minute
38 seconds

Josh
2 minutes
7 seconds

Becky
3 minutes
9 seconds

Karim
2 minutes
47 seconds

Billy
2 minutes
31 seconds

1   Write the times in order, quickest to slowest.

1. 1 minute 38 seconds, 1 minute 54 seconds, ...

Who was: 2   4th   3   last   4   6th

Which children finished the race in:

5   more than 150 seconds   6   less than 130 seconds

7   between 100 and 150 seconds   8   between 160 and 180 seconds

Write the times in order, shortest to longest.

9   1 minute, $\frac{1}{2}$ minute, 40 seconds, 1 minute 25 seconds

10 85 seconds, 1 minute 20 seconds, $1\frac{1}{2}$ minutes, 95 seconds

11 2 minutes 20 seconds, 125 seconds, 2 minutes 35 seconds, 145 seconds

Estimate how long 1000 seconds is in minutes.
Work it out. How close were you? Try 2000 seconds.

Seconds

These are the tracks on the new CD by Mathkidz.

Mathkidz

Track 1	*It all adds up*	2 minutes 55 seconds
Track 2	*Count on me*	3 minutes 10 seconds
Track 3	*She's double trouble*	1 minute 48 seconds
Track 4	*Polygon blues*	2 minutes 37 seconds
Track 5	*You're odd, I'm even*	3 minutes 5 seconds
Track 6	*You can draw my graph*	4 minutes 2 seconds
Track 7	*Don't take me away*	2 minutes 45 seconds
Track 8	*No difference*	3 minutes 35 seconds
Track 9	*Here's my number*	1 minute 25 seconds
Track 10	*You're so square*	3 minutes 11 seconds

Write how many seconds these tracks last:

1. 2 1 5 seconds

1   No difference
2   You can draw my graph
3   Polygon blues
4   Count on me
5   You're so square
6   It all adds up

Write how long for:

7   the first three tracks
8   the first five tracks
9   the last two tracks
10 the last five tracks

Write these times in seconds:

11. 1 0 5 seconds

11 1 minute 45 seconds
12 2 minutes 38 seconds
13 3 minutes 16 seconds
14 4 minutes 9 seconds
15 1 minute 58 seconds
16 2 minutes 17 seconds
17 10 minutes 20 seconds
18 5 minutes 35 seconds

Think of three tracks on your favourite CD. How long do they last altogether? Write the number of seconds.

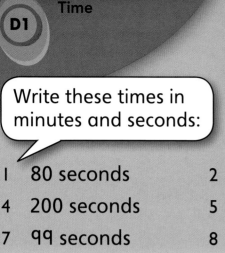

Write these times in minutes and seconds:

1. 1 minute 20 seconds

1   80 seconds   2   115 seconds   3   135 seconds

4   200 seconds   5   400 seconds   6   193 seconds

7   99 seconds   8   217 seconds   9   670 seconds

10   Harriet Postlethwaite-Smith can write her name in 10 seconds. How many times can she write her name in $2\frac{1}{2}$ minutes?

11   A team of four ran a relay race. Gary took 43 seconds, Pete took 55 seconds, Neelaksh took 38 seconds and Matt took 62 seconds. The record for the race is 3 minutes 15 seconds. How far short of the record are they?

12   Sally made three phone calls which lasted 3 minutes 15 seconds, 6 minutes 45 seconds and 5 minutes 30 seconds. Calls cost 6p per minute. How much did her calls cost?

Explore

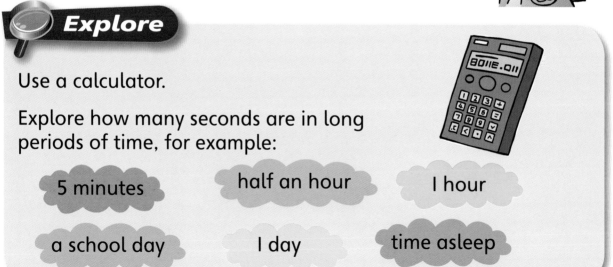

Use a calculator.

Explore how many seconds are in long periods of time, for example:

5 minutes   half an hour   1 hour

a school day   1 day   time asleep

2s, 3s, 4s, 5s, 10s

Write the next four multiples in each list.

1. 1 2, 1 4, 1 6, 1 8

1   2   4   6   8   10

2   3   6   9   12   15

3   4   8   12   16

4   5   10   15   20   25

5   10   20   30   40

How many multiples of 2 under 50 are there? How about multiples of 3? 4? 5?

6   Write the multiples of 5.   Write the multiples of 10.   Which numbers are in both lists?

31	32	33	34	35	36	37	38	39	40
41	42	43	44	45	46	47	48	49	50
51	52	53	54	55	56	57	58	59	60
61	62	63	64	65	66	67	68	69	70

7   Write the multiples of 2.   Write the multiples of 3.   Which numbers are in both lists?

1	2	3	4	5	6	7	8	9	10
11	12	13	14	15	16	17	18	19	20
21	22	23	24	25	26	27	28	29	30

Multiples

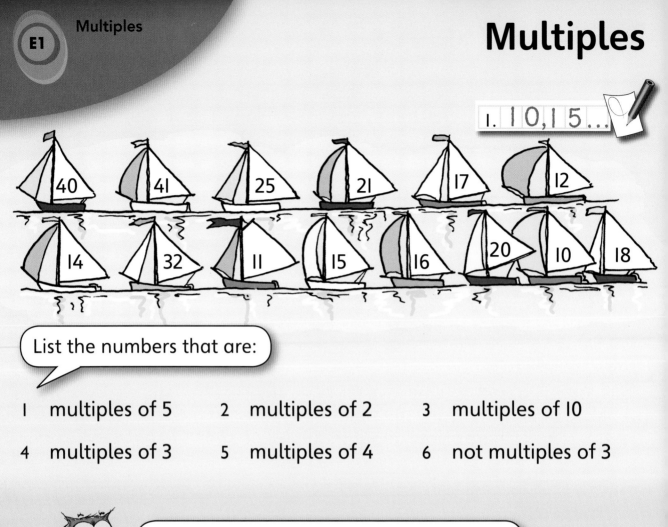

1. 10, 15...

List the numbers that are:

1   multiples of 5   2   multiples of 2   3   multiples of 10

4   multiples of 3   5   multiples of 4   6   not multiples of 3

Write eight numbers greater than 10 that are not multiples of 2 nor multiples of 3.

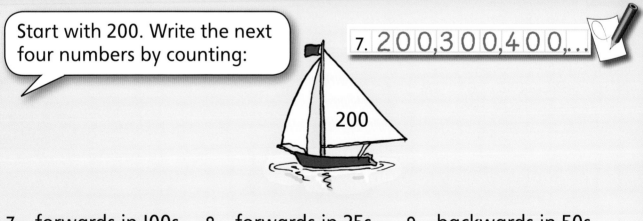

Start with 200. Write the next four numbers by counting:

7. 200, 300, 400, ...

7   forwards in 100s   8   forwards in 25s   9   backwards in 50s

10   forwards in 200s   11   backwards in 10s   12   forwards in 2s

13   forwards in 50s   14   backwards in 25s   15   backwards in 2s

Multiples

1. 2 8, 3 0 ...

After each number write the next:

1 multiple of 2   2 multiple of 10   3 multiple of 5

4 multiple of 25   5 multiple of 150

Write three multiples of 25 which are not multiples of 50. Ask your partner to do the same. What do you notice?

Explore

The multiples of 4 are: 4 8 12 16 20 24 28 32 36 ...

Their units' digits are: 4 8 2 6 0 4 8 2 6 ...

Describe any patterns you can see.
Look for patterns in the units digits of multiples of other numbers.

Multiples

True or false?

1 All multiples of 4 are also multiples of 2.
2 All multiples of 5 are also multiples of 10.
3 All multiples of 2 are even numbers.
4 All multiples of 3 are odd numbers.
5 12 is a multiple of 2, 3, and 4.
6 All numbers which are multiples of 4 and 5 are multiples of 10.

I point for a multiple of 2
2 points for a multiple of 5
3 points for a multiple of 3

7.   1 6 = 1 point
       2 1 = 3 points
   total = 4 points

Write each overall score.

7 | 16 | 13 | 21 | 17 |

8 | 25 | 11 | 9 | 14 |

9 | 7 | 11 | 13 | 17 |

10 | 26 | 23 | 35 | 21 |

11 | 27 | 7 | 4 | 3 |

12 | 19 | 35 | 8 | 28 |

Write the smallest number that is:

13 a multiple of 2 and a multiple of 5
14 a multiple of 3 and a multiple of 2
15 a multiple of 5 and a multiple of 25
16 a multiple of 50 and a multiple of 100
17 a multiple of 4 and a multiple of 5
18 a multiple of 10 and a multiple of 25

CANDY FLOSS

Multiplication facts

Write the position of the pointer on each counting stick.

1. (a) 6

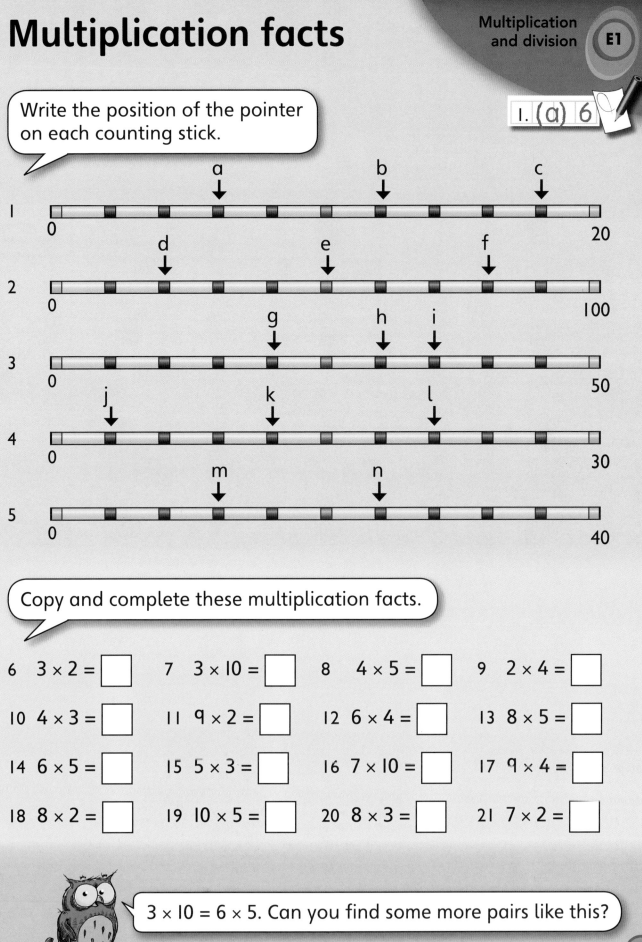

Copy and complete these multiplication facts.

6 $3 \times 2 = \boxed{}$ 7 $3 \times 10 = \boxed{}$ 8 $4 \times 5 = \boxed{}$ 9 $2 \times 4 = \boxed{}$

10 $4 \times 3 = \boxed{}$ 11 $9 \times 2 = \boxed{}$ 12 $6 \times 4 = \boxed{}$ 13 $8 \times 5 = \boxed{}$

14 $6 \times 5 = \boxed{}$ 15 $5 \times 3 = \boxed{}$ 16 $7 \times 10 = \boxed{}$ 17 $9 \times 4 = \boxed{}$

18 $8 \times 2 = \boxed{}$ 19 $10 \times 5 = \boxed{}$ 20 $8 \times 3 = \boxed{}$ 21 $7 \times 2 = \boxed{}$

$3 \times 10 = 6 \times 5$. Can you find some more pairs like this?

Multiplication and division facts

Complete these division facts. You can use the multiplication square to help you.

1. $18 \div 2 = 9$

1 $18 \div 2 = \boxed{}$ 2 $25 \div 5 = \boxed{}$

3 $70 \div 10 = \boxed{}$ 4 $15 \div 3 = \boxed{}$

5 $20 \div 4 = \boxed{}$ 6 $14 \div 2 = \boxed{}$

7 $35 \div 5 = \boxed{}$ 8 $21 \div 3 = \boxed{}$

9 $32 \div 4 = \boxed{}$ 10 $45 \div 5 = \boxed{}$

11 $24 \div 6 = \boxed{}$ 12 $24 \div 8 = \boxed{}$

1	2	3	4	5	6	7	8	9	10
2	4	6	8	10	12	14	16	18	20
3	6	9	12	15	18	21	24	27	30
4	8	12	16	20	24	28	32	36	40
5	10	15	20	25	30	35	40	45	50
6	12	18	24	30	36	42	48	54	60
7	14	21	28	35	42	49	56	63	70
8	16	24	32	40	48	56	64	72	80
9	18	27	36	45	54	63	72	81	90
10	20	30	40	50	60	70	80	90	100

Which numbers less than 30 have a remainder when divided by 3? Which have a remainder of 2?

For each multiplication, write two matching divisions.

13. $14 \div 2 = 7, \quad 14 \div 7 = 2$

13 $7 \times 2 = 14$ 14 $3 \times 5 = 15$ 15 $6 \times 3 = 18$ 16 $7 \times 4 = 28$

For each division, write two matching multiplications.

17. $4 \times 5 = 20, \quad 5 \times 4 = 20$

17 $20 \div 4 = 5$ 18 $12 \div 3 = 4$ 19 $8 \div 2 = 4$ 20 $50 \div 10 = 5$

Multiplication and division facts

Copy and complete these multiplication and division facts.

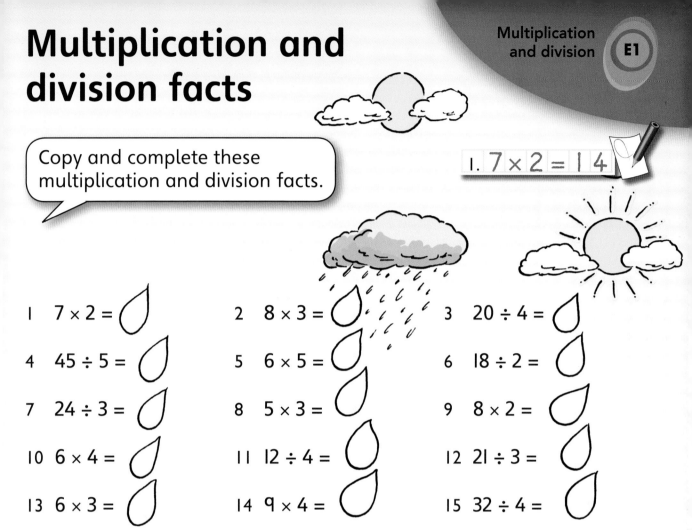

1. $7 \times 2 = 14$

1 $7 \times 2 =$

2 $8 \times 3 =$

3 $20 \div 4 =$

4 $45 \div 5 =$

5 $6 \times 5 =$

6 $18 \div 2 =$

7 $24 \div 3 =$

8 $5 \times 3 =$

9 $8 \times 2 =$

10 $6 \times 4 =$

11 $12 \div 4 =$

12 $21 \div 3 =$

13 $6 \times 3 =$

14 $9 \times 4 =$

15 $32 \div 4 =$

Explore

Use a multiplication square.

Make a blue rainbow by colouring all the 20s.
Call this the 20-rainbow.

Make the 18-rainbow using a different colour.

Explore different rainbows you could make.

1	2	3	4	5	6	7	8	9	10
2	4	6	8	10	12	14	16	18	20
3	6	9	12	15	18	21	24	27	30
4	8	12	16	20	24	28	32	36	40
5	10	15	20	25	30	35	40	45	50
6	12	18	24	30	36	42	48	54	60
7	14	21	28	35	42	44	56	63	70
8	16	24	32	40	48	56	64	72	80
9	18	27	36	45	54	63	72	81	90
10	20	30	40	50	60	70	80	90	100

Multiplication and division facts

Find the secret numbers.

1 Two numbers multiply together to make 18. One number is half the other. What is the smaller number?

2 What number divided by 3 gives the number of days in a week?

3 A number multiplied by itself gives an answer between 10 and 20. What is the number?

4 Divide the number of months in a year by the number of seasons in a year, and then multiply the answer by itself.

5 Multiply the number of sides of a hexagon by the number of corners of a pentagon, then divide the answer by the number of sides of a decagon.

6 Divide the number of centimetres in half a metre by the number of millimetres in a centimetre, then multiply the answer by itself.

7 Divide 3 by itself, then multiply the answer by itself.

Find the missing numbers.

8. $6 \times 3 = 18$

8 $6 \times \bigcirc = 18$

9 $\bigcirc \div 2 = 7$

10 $\bigcirc \times 5 = 35$

11 $30 \div \bigcirc = 6$

12 $\bigcirc \div 4 = 8$

13 $\bigcirc \times 10 = 70$

14 $5 \times \bigcirc = 20$

15 $\bigcirc \div 3 = 7$

16 $9 \times \bigcirc = 18$

17 $7 \times \bigcirc = 28$

18 $12 \div \bigcirc = 6$

19 $9 \times \bigcirc = 27$

Invent five missing number facts for which the missing number is always 3. Try them out on your partner.

Fractions

For each set of candles, write the fraction of red candles.

1. $\dfrac{3}{4}$

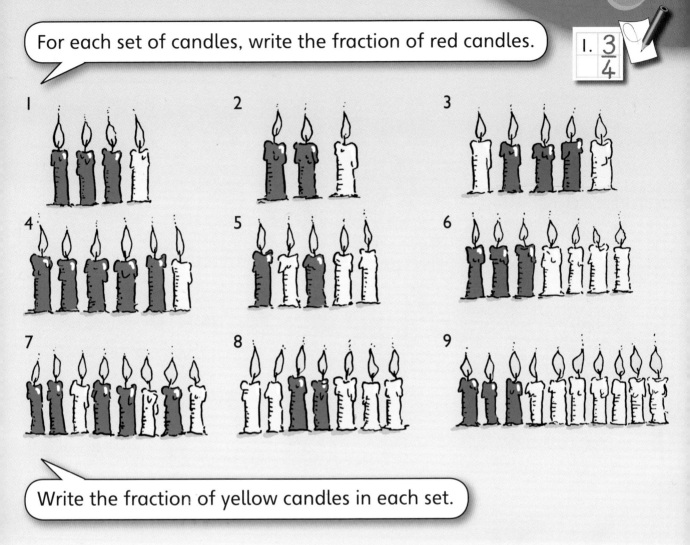

1

2

3

4

5

6

7

8

9

Write the fraction of yellow candles in each set.

Explore

Use up to 6 counters, which can be red or yellow.

Explore how many different fractions of red counters you can show. Record each one with a picture and a fraction.

 $\dfrac{5}{6}$

 $\dfrac{1}{4}$

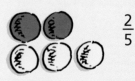 $\dfrac{2}{5}$

Mixed numbers

How many cakes?

1. $2\frac{1}{4}$

1

2

3

4

5

6

7

8

9

There were five of each kind of cake.
How much has been eaten each time?

How many quarters?

10. $1\frac{1}{4} = \frac{5}{4}$

10 $1\frac{1}{4}$ 11 $2\frac{3}{4}$ 12 $3\frac{1}{4}$ 13 5

How many thirds?

14 $1\frac{2}{3}$ 15 $3\frac{1}{3}$ 16 $5\frac{2}{3}$ 17 3

How many fifths?

18 $1\frac{3}{5}$ 19 $2\frac{1}{5}$ 20 $3\frac{4}{5}$ 21 $6\frac{3}{5}$

Mixed numbers

Write the number of towers in each set.

1. $1\frac{3}{4}$

1 2 3 4 5 6

Write the number of cubes in these sets of towers:

7 8 9

10 11 12

Use 11 cubes. Make different mixed numbers.

Draw these towers of 5 cubes:

13.

13 $1\frac{2}{5}$ 14 $2\frac{1}{5}$ 15 $3\frac{4}{5}$

Draw these towers of 4 cubes:

16 $2\frac{1}{4}$ 17 $1\frac{3}{4}$ 18 $3\frac{1}{2}$

Mixed numbers

Each ferry trip takes $\frac{1}{4}$ hour. How many hours for:

1. $1\frac{3}{4}$

1   7 trips   2   5 trips   3   19 trips   4   43 trips

Each rowing boat trip takes $\frac{1}{2}$ hour. How many hours for:

5   11 trips   6   34 trips   7   29 trips   8   17 trips

Each punt trip takes $\frac{1}{3}$ hour. How many hours for:

9   10 trips   10 20 trips   11 62 trips   12 26 trips

How many trips can each boat make in 8 hours?

Change each fraction to a mixed number.

13. $3\frac{1}{3}$

13 $\frac{10}{3}$ 14 $\frac{7}{4}$ 15 $\frac{5}{2}$ 16 $\frac{9}{5}$ 17 $\frac{23}{10}$ 18 $\frac{8}{7}$

19 $\frac{21}{2}$ 20 $\frac{31}{5}$ 21 $\frac{111}{10}$ 22 $\frac{62}{5}$ 23 $\frac{13}{6}$ 24 $\frac{21}{8}$

Matching fractions

Write the pairs of shaded fractions.

1. $\frac{1}{2} = \frac{2}{4}$

1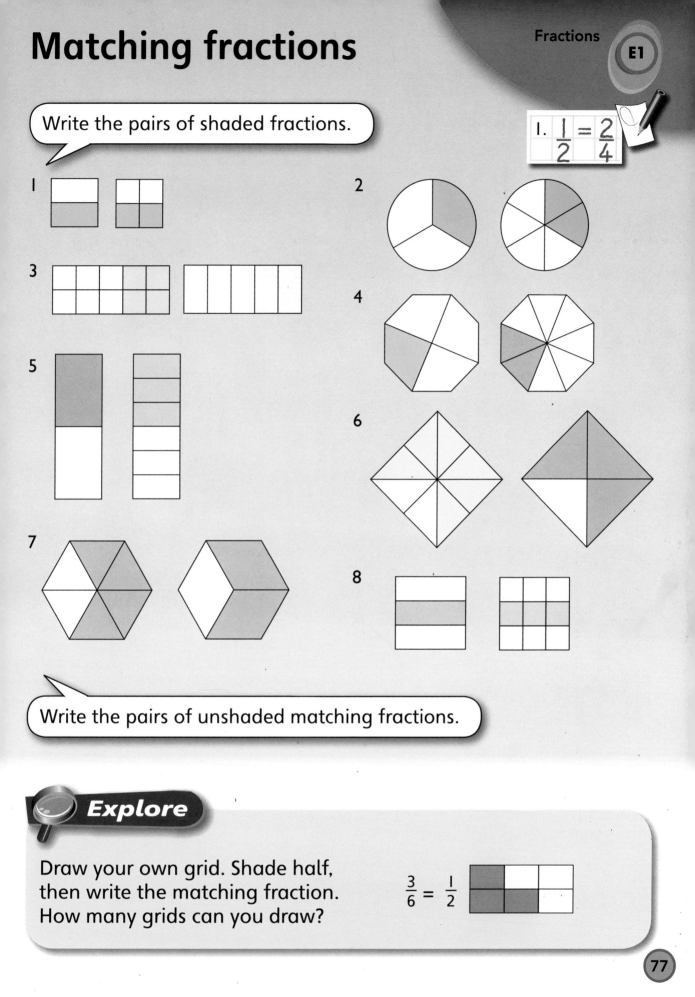

2

3

4

5

6

7

8

Write the pairs of unshaded matching fractions.

Explore

Draw your own grid. Shade half, then write the matching fraction. How many grids can you draw?

$\frac{3}{6} = \frac{1}{2}$

Matching fractions

Sort these into pairs of matching coloured fractions. Write the pairs and their fractions.

$$a = \frac{4}{8}, g = \frac{1}{2}$$

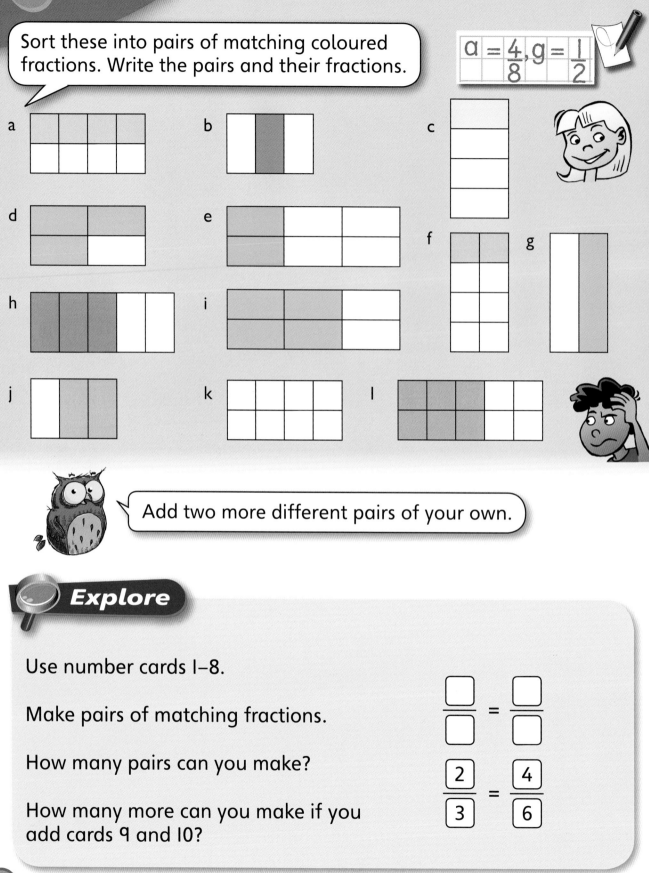

a

b

c

d

e

f

g

h

i

j

k

l

Add two more different pairs of your own.

Explore

Use number cards 1–8.

Make pairs of matching fractions.

How many pairs can you make?

How many more can you make if you add cards 9 and 10?

$$\frac{\square}{\square} = \frac{\square}{\square}$$

$$\frac{2}{3} = \frac{4}{6}$$

Matching fractions

> Complete these pairs of matching fractions.
> Use the fraction walls to help you.

1. $\dfrac{1}{2} = \dfrac{2}{4}$

1. $\dfrac{1}{2} = \dfrac{\square}{4}$

2. $\dfrac{2}{4} = \dfrac{\square}{8}$

3. $\dfrac{2}{2} = \dfrac{\square}{4}$

4. $\dfrac{6}{8} = \dfrac{\square}{4}$

5. $\dfrac{1}{2} = \dfrac{\square}{8}$

6. $1 = \dfrac{\square}{4}$

7. $\dfrac{1}{3} = \dfrac{\square}{6}$

8. $\dfrac{\square}{3} = \dfrac{4}{6}$

9. $\dfrac{3}{6} = \dfrac{\square}{12}$

10. $\dfrac{\square}{3} = \dfrac{8}{12}$

11. $\dfrac{1}{3} = \dfrac{\square}{12}$

12. $\dfrac{\square}{3} = \dfrac{6}{6}$

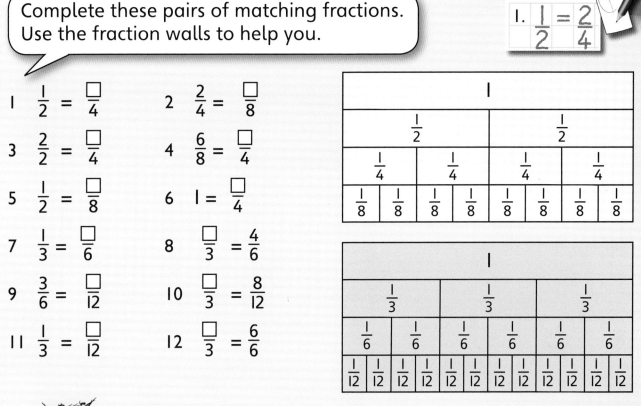

> The bottom of my fraction wall is
> divided into $\frac{1}{20}$s. Draw the whole wall.

13 There were 16 cyclists on a trip. Half of them stay in a hostel,
and a quarter of them camp. How many go home for the night?

14 Class 4 has 30 children. Half have packed lunches.
One sixth go home. What fraction have school
dinners? How many children is this?

15 James had 12 marbles. Two sixths were
red, one third were blue, the rest were
green. What fraction was green?

Matching fractions

Each fraction has a matching partner. Write the pairs. Who has no partner?

1. $\frac{1}{2}$ and $\frac{2}{4}$

Find the odd one out in each list.

2 $\frac{1}{2}, \frac{5}{10}, \frac{2}{4}, \frac{4}{6}$ 3 $\frac{1}{3}, \frac{2}{6}, \frac{6}{12}, \frac{3}{9}$ 4 $\frac{2}{8}, \frac{2}{6}, \frac{1}{4}, \frac{3}{12}$

5 $\frac{9}{12}, \frac{3}{4}, \frac{2}{3}, \frac{6}{8}$ 6 $\frac{1}{5}, \frac{20}{100}, \frac{2}{10}, \frac{6}{20}$ 7 $\frac{2}{3}, \frac{6}{9}, \frac{4}{6}, \frac{3}{4}$